P9-DIA-381

ALBERT CAMUS
and
CHRISTIANITY

PQ 2605 .A3734 Z72313
Onimus, Jean.
Albert Camus and
  Christianity.

ALBERT CAMUS
and
CHRISTIANITY

by

JEAN ONIMUS

Translated by EMMETT PARKER

UNIVERSITY OF ALABAMA PRESS
University, Alabama

RITTER LIBRARY
BALDWIN-WALLACE COLLEGE
WITHDRAWN

Translated into English from *Camus*, Copyright © 1965
by Desclée De Brouwer

English translation and translator's addenda Copyright © 1970
by University of Alabama Press
Standard Book Number: 8173-7601-1
Library of Congress Catalog Card Number: 77-92654
Manufactured in the United States of America

Table of Contents

Abbreviations   vi
Translator's Preface   ix
Introduction   3
1. The Kingdom and the Exile   7
   The Kingdom   7
   Exile   18
2. No to God   31
3. An Atheistic Humanism   64
   The Temptation of Nihilism   64
   Positive Values   77
   A Conscience in Quest of its Judge   91
4. A Great Unfulfilled Love   102
   Texts   107
   Chronology   144
   Select Bibliography   149
   Index   157

Abbreviations Used

in Textual References

All English translations of quotations from Camus's writings, unless otherwise indicated, are my own; in these cases, I have given page references to the original French texts. I have bracketed below the English titles of works by Camus that have been translated to date; full references to these may be found in the Select Bibliography at the back of the book. Page references to works marked with an asterisk are to the Pléiade edition of Camus's writings [trans. note].

A/I,* A/III*   *Actuelles*, vols. I and III. [A selection from vols. I and II (the latter is not cited in this study) of Camus's collected articles may be found in *Resistance, Rebellion and Death*.]

CL*   *Caligula.*

CN   *Carnets: mai 1935–février 1942* [*Notebooks*].

EE   *L'Envers et l'endroit* [*The Right and the Wrong Side*].

*ER**	*L'Exil et le royaume* [*Exile and the Kingdom*].
ET	*L'Etranger* [*The Stranger*].
Eté	*L'Eté* [*Summer*].
HR	*L'Homme révolté* [*The Rebel*].
*LA**	*Lettres à un ami allemand* [*Letters to a German Friend*].
*LC**	*La Chute* [*The Fall*].
*LM**	*Le Malentendu* [*Cross-purposes*].
*LP**	*La Peste* [*The Plague*].
MS	*Le Mythe de Sisyphe* [*The Myth of Sisyphus*]
P/I, PL/II**	The Pléiade edition of Camus's works, vols. I and II. [These are used only to refer to certain supplementary documents contained in appendices to this edition.]

Translator's Preface

This book is a valuable addition to the body of Camus criticism in English, and is especially useful as an exemplification of an important and influential current of critical interpretation—that of the more traditional Christian commentators, especially the French Roman Catholic ones—not hitherto readily available to English-language students of Camus's works. *Albert Camus and Christianity* will undoubtedly arouse controversy—rather, it will continue a controversy that haunted Camus during his lifetime and continues to this day. It is absolutely beyond doubt that Camus was an atheist; but because he was not militantly antireligious—he remarked in an interview (*Le Monde*, 1956) that he found "in irreligiousness something . . . yes, something trite"—and because certain of his philosophical preoccupations often parallel those of Christianity, Camus and his work have rarely met with the open hostility that a less compromising—and less tolerant—atheist such as Sartre has experienced.

The controversy does not center around whether Camus was an atheist, however, but rather around the meaning and direction of his thought, in which his disbelief plays a vital role. For Christian critics of an essentially Augustinian cast, Camus's work ultimately affirms the total helplessness of man without a Divine intercessor. Some Christian critics have seemed to suggest, if indirectly, that Camus might well have been converted to Christianity but for his untimely death in an automobile accident. Other critics less firmly wedded to the fundamental tenets of Christianity—the divinity of Christ, concepts of original sin, doctrines of grace, etc.—see in his work, on the contrary, an affirmation of both man's admitted limitations and the large potential of his solitary humanity.

The work of any writer is of course open to differing interpretations. This is especially so in Camus's case because of a certain opaqueness and ambiguity in such works as *L'Étranger* and *La Chute*, and because the moral concerns implicit in all his works are often close to those professed by representatives of the very institutions and groups about which Camus had serious reservations. (Thus, for example, Sartre and Francis Jeanson in 1952, quoting out of context, had no great difficulty in castigating *L'Homme révolté* for giving "aid and comfort" to a supposedly uneasy bourgeois conscience.) It is inevitable, moreover, that any critic's treatment of a writer's work will reflect some of the critic's own preconceptions. I have devoted some study to Camus's role as writer and thinker, and I have some strong reservations concerning certain of M. Onimus's analyses and comments. Casual readers who are unaware of certain long-standing theological controversies in France and have little or no access to French-language sources might wish to supplement their reading of M. Onimus's essay with certain other studies of Camus, diversely oriented, that express complementary or even divergent views: Germaine Brée's *Camus*, John Cruickshank's *Albert Camus and the Literature of Revolt*, Philip Thody's *Camus: 1913–1960*, Thomas

Hanna's *The Thought and Art of Albert Camus*, and especially the English translation of Roger Quilliot's just-revised *La Mer et les prisons*, which is to be published later this year by the University of Alabama Press.

While the response of some Christian critics to Camus tends to be ambiguous, divided, as it is likely to be, between admiration and mistrust of a man whose ethical concerns they share but whose indifference to the fundamental doctrines of Christian faith they can neither fully appreciate nor reconcile with their perception of his personality and his thought, we don't know to what extent they represent the majority of Christians. However, they are sufficiently numerous to raise a serious question about the depth of Camus's effective influence—in Christian circles, at least—as a persuasive analyst of contemporary man's predicament.

In one of the short stories in *L'Exil et le royaume* (*Exile and the Kingdom*) Jonas, a painter, who has retreated into his attic to escape the hangers-on and admirers whose eternal presence make it impossible for him to work, hands down a blank canvas in the center of which a single word has been written in very small letters—so small that even on close examination it is impossible to be certain whether the word is *solitaire* or *solidaire*, solitude or solidarity.* This incident is a humorously ironic treatment of the artist's dilemma: how to reconcile the need for solitude that his work requires with the need to participate in the everyday life of his time so that his work will not become divorced from reality.

But, as Camus's own work emphasizes, this dilemma is not the artist's alone. For in our age men are seemingly more

* "Jonas ou l'artiste au travail," *Théâtre, Récits, Nouvelles* (Paris: Editions de la Pléiade, 1962), p. 1652.

alone than they have ever been before—more separated
from one another by conflicting ideologies and aspirations
than ever before—and yet they are more dependent on each
other for their very survival and that of the planet. In one
sense there is really no choice left between solitude and
solidarity. Certainly physical solidarity, at least, is imposed
on us. Like it or not, we all live today in an often uncom-
fortable, but unavoidable, proximity to the rest of the human
race. How to parlay that physical proximity into a produc-
tive solidarity of human purpose is one of contemporary
man's dilemmas. As a first step toward extricating ourselves
from the impasse of enforced confrontation, Camus felt that
a genuine dialogue had to be established among men of conflicting ideas.

Immediately after World War II Camus, as an editorialist
for the Parisian daily *Combat*, attempted to open such a
dialogue between himself and representatives in France of
two of the world's major ideologies, the Christians and the
Communists. He soon abandoned his overtures to the latter,
convinced that they could not or would not discuss any
issue outside the context of a hard Marxist-Leninist line. He
was somewhat more hopeful with regard to Christians. He
had been deeply impressed by Catholic comrades he had
met in the Resistance, and most especially by his close friend
the Catholic poet René Leynaud, who was killed by the
Milices, the French collaborationist arm of the Gestapo,
just before the liberation of Paris. Camus sensed that a
certain common ground existed between Christians and
those unbelievers like himself who were animated by a
strong sense of human justice, and he hoped that they could
join forces against the rising tide of oppression he saw
threatening whatever vestige of human freedom was left in

western Europe. Thus, in an address before the Dominican community of Latour–Maubourg in Paris, he pleaded with Christians to join "a handful of lonely men who today, without any faith or law, plead ceaselessly and nearly everywhere for children and for men."*

To some extent, many Christians responded. A number of liberal Catholics in France and elsewhere, as well as many Protestants, have enthusiastically embraced Camus's thought, recognizing in him a kindred spirit of social justice despite his repeatedly professed inability to accept their theological positions. Yet one cannot but wonder whether any real communication—true dialogue—was ever established between Camus and the majority of orthodox Christians familiar with his thought.

Camus has much to offer the world. It is important to both Christians and non-Christians that the full implications of his thought be understood. It is not too late to establish the kind of dialogue Camus called for—a free and sincere exchange between men with a keen sense of justice and human compassion willing to break down the ideologically imposed barriers of solitude that may separate us. This book represents a sincere effort to respond to Camus's appeal, and much of its value lies in the clarity of its response. It is the responsibility of every man of good will to take up and continually expand the dialogue. If this does not occur, then Camus's own dire prediction may well come true for all of us: "It is possible, and moreover most probable, that Christianity will stubbornly cling to compromise, or indeed to pronouncing condemnations in the obscure language of

* "L'Incroyant et les Chrétiens," *Essais* (Paris: Editions de la Pléiade, 1965), p. 375.

encyclicals. It is possible that it will resist letting finally
being brought forth the virtue of revolt and indignation
which, a long time ago now, it possessed. Then Christians
will live on and Christianity will die." (*Essais*, p. 375.)

University, Alabama   EMMETT PARKER
December, 1969

ALBERT CAMUS
and
CHRISTIANITY

Introduction

> "Anxiety and even terror, if it is sincere, is good; spellbound faith, on the other hand, is bad."
> —Péguy, *Œuvres en Prose*, I, 157

Because he was not a philosopher but a simple man endowed with the genius of expression, Camus is close to all of us and is all the more engaging a witness by virtue of his not being excessively gifted in the use of dialectics and the spirit of synthesis. The philosopher, playing his intellectual games, can stand apart and look down upon the crowd; abstract thought alienates itself from everything by the very act of clarifying it. Camus knew neither that illumination nor that refuge. He was jostled by everyday events like all of us, and his thought encountered all the clashes of our recent history. That thought remains open and unfinished; no one can say what it might have become in maturing.

In contrast to those doctrinaire spokesmen of our era, believers in the righteousness of their ideologies, Camus remained a man who always sought and who was never certain, but whose every hesitation engages us by its frankness and severity. "I am not a philosopher," he told an interviewer in 1945. "I do not have enough faith in reason to believe in a system. What concerns me is to know how to decide one's conduct when one believes neither in God nor in Reason." In this way Camus lived the "heart of the matter," through stripping away the unessential and through candid simplicity, because he was a child of this century and knew to the fullest its wretchedness and its virtues.

Can this "heart of the matter" be termed "religious"? Here we must take care and weigh our words. In the strict sense, if one understands by religion the sense of the divine, and the myths, dogmas, and liturgies that grow out of it, we must say unequivocally that Camus was totally divorced from religion. For him the question was outmoded, resolved long ago. This was a point on which this man, who was often changeable, never varied: there is not the slightest trace of "formal" religion in him. But there is in him the trace of a scar, even an open wound, precisely that which occurs in every lucid consciousness in the wake of "the death of God." The "heart of the problem" in Camus is "religious" if one refers by this term to what is at the origin of religions: existential anguish, the sense of guilt, the horror of death, the atrocious experience of the Absurd. If the man of our times is no longer religious, he remains, he even becomes more than ever a tragic man because he feels himself caught between two fatalities that destroy him: the fatality imposed on him by nature and the fatality that he himself creates and which he calls History. "The world that the individual of the eighteenth century thought he could subjugate and form through reason and science has taken on in fact a definite form, but its form is monstrous. Rational and at the same time incoherent, it is the world of

History. But, at this level of incoherence, History has taken on the face of Destiny. Man doubts his power to dominate it, he can only struggle against it. A curious paradox: humanity, with the very tools used to reject fatality, has carved out for itself a hostile fate. *After having made a god of the reign of humanity, man turns once more against this new god* . . . This contradictory creature, henceforth conscious of the ambiguity of man and his history, this creature is the tragic man par excellence" (P/I, p. 1707). We have italicized above a sentence which sums up the drama of atheistic humanism and of Camus himself. Camus was to make a courageous effort to go beyond the contradiction and to open our perspective upon a new form of wisdom that would permit men to remain worthy of the name man, while doing without God, in order to render the irrational less opaque and even to make of it a paradoxical foundation stone of heroism and sainthood. It is important for all, believers and unbelievers alike, to see if he succeeded. Is an orphaned humanism possible? The very fact that a reading of Camus poses such a question shows what level this artist, this "outsider," reached. The Nobel Prize was awarded him for that, because his work "sheds light on the problems which in our time confronts men's consciences." What one sought to honor in him was the witness for a generation cantilevered between the decadence of an outworn order and fear of the future that men are building and that many see, forebodingly, as more inhuman than ever.

J. O.

1

The Kingdom
and the Exile

The Kingdom

Camus was first of all—and remained essentially so all his life—a Mediterranean. That is to say his attention was first drawn and held by the beauty of sky and sea, physical pleasures, and the flowering of the simplest kind of happiness. Greek thought has always turned away from the kind of subjectivity that closes in upon itself and claims to make the universe depend upon its self-derived experience. Descartes shut himself up in a cell like Rembrandt's *Philosopher*, and only when he shut his eyes did he come face to face with Being. All of western philosophy grows out of this inclination—this philosophy of human pride, which is the creator and transformer of a world that it engenders through thought, and which is a tragic philosophy because it separates man from the universe in which he lives. For Camus, born in Algiers, the authentic realities were, first of all, almond trees in bloom, swimming in the sea, the softness of summer evenings. His first gods were given him along with the beauty of the world; offering himself to the sun or contemplating the night radiant with stars sufficed to convince him that the world was replete. There are countries where the eyes of men, once opened, are as though surfeited. The hero of *La Chute* (*The Fall*), Clamence, is a Parisian, and it is in the fog and dirty snow of the port of Amsterdam that he pours out his bad conscience; but Meursault, the hero of *L'Etranger* (*The Stranger*), a man who has no conscience, a man for whom things are only what they are and who lives outside himself in the present moment, is a native of Algiers. Camus at the outset was as "innocent" as Meursault, his creation, and later, after western philosophy had unsealed Camus' inner vision, he felt a continuous nostalgia for that original innocence and the memory of that earlier plenitude. Camus felt himself an exile, driven out of his paradise by the demons of a spirit that was not of his own native land. And whatever confusion and disappointment he may have experienced in the course of his life, he found even at the darkest moments a source of joy in the recaptured wind of Tipasa,* in the harmony of a landscape at Vicenza or Fiesole, in the waves breaking on the beach, in the summertime, and especially in the African sun when it filled the heavens with its rays.

That innocence, that ingenuous contact with the elements, that happy participation in the beauty of the world preserved more than immediate life and interior unity. Through an unexpected twist, his cosmic contemplation showed itself capable of leading to a veritable religious ecstasy because it filled and saturated all the desires of the

---

* Tipasa: a small resort town some thirty miles west of Algiers, the site of Roman ruins; "Noces à Tipasa" ("Nuptials at Tipasa") is the title of the first essay in *Noces* [trans. note].

soul. "The silent contemplation of a landscape," writes Jean Grenier, "suffices to silence desire. The void is immediately replaced by fullness."* It was in fact to Grenier, who was his professor of philosophy for two years, that Camus owed the confirmation and, if one may say so, the authentication of his cosmic instinct. At noon, at the Villa Floridiana in Naples, Grenier experienced less "a sentiment of happiness than a sentiment *of real and total presence*, as if all the fissures of being were sealed"**—a very concrete and even striking expression of that plenitude suggested by the life of innocence mentioned above. To make of happy existence something solid, a compact block, by bringing it into perfect accord with the perceptible harmony around us and thus extinguish the desire for escape, obliterate the apprehension of death and of nothingness, to cease to see misfortune . . . Camus found another example of such an experience in Dostoevski. How deeply he was influenced by Kirillov in *The Possessed* is known;*** it was he who first posed for Camus the problem of suicide; but he also revealed to him those epileptic ecstasies so frequent in the works of the Russian novelist: "There are seconds," Kirillov says to Shatov, "—they come five or six at a time—when you suddenly feel the presence of the eternal harmony perfectly attained. It's something not earthly—I don't mean in the sense that it's heavenly—but in the sense that man cannot endure it in his earthly aspect. He must be

* Jean Grenier, *Les Iles* (Paris, 1959), p. 29.
** *Les Iles*, p. 90.
*** Camus wrote an adaptation of Fëdor Dostoevski's *The Possessed* for the stage (see *Théâtre, Récits, Nouvelles*, pp. 921–1117), which he directed himself; the first performance was given in Paris at the Théâtre Antoine on January 30, 1959 [trans. note].

physically changed or die. This feeling is clear and unmistakable; it's as though you apprehend all nature and suddenly say, 'Yes, that's right.' "* Elsewhere Kirillov describes to Stavrogin a leaf, "a leaf from a tree . . . . When I was ten years old I used to shut my eyes in the winter on purpose and fancy a green leaf, bright, with veins on it, and the sun shining . . . I'm not speaking of an allegory, but of a leaf, only a leaf. The leaf is good. Everything's good . . . . Man is unhappy because he doesn't know he's happy. It's only that. That's all, that's all! If anyone finds out he'll become happy at once, that minute."** One wonders if the whole of Camus's "metaphysics" did not come from some such text. Does not his humanism, of which we will speak further on, consist in delivering men from fear and rendering to them a happiness they already possess without knowing it? Let us recall again the dream that Versilov recounts in *A Raw Youth:* men have lost their belief in God, in the immortality of the soul, and "all the wealth of love lavished of old upon Him, who was immortal. . . ."*** Then they turn that love toward nature, the world, men, each blade of grass. And it was certainly, in fact, the sentiment of finality, the evidence of death, and his atheism that firmly oriented Camus toward nature; it filled the abyss that consciousness creates, it was God Himself rendered visible to the senses. Nature snatches the conscious being from his subjectivity and overwhelms him suddenly by annihilating him, an experience well known to the mystics. "That landscape," Camus wrote, "placed me

* Fëdor Dostoevski, *The Possessed*, trans. Constance Garnett (New York, 1963), p. 601.
** *The Possessed*, p. 240.
*** Fëdor Dostoevski, *A Raw Youth*, trans. Constance Garnett (New York, 1961), pp. 510–11.

outside myself . . . ." It taught him "that the spirit is
nothing, nor even the heart itself" (*N*, p. 96). An ambiguous experience in which the contemplator experiences himself as nothingness and as totality, by turns, in which the
external world becomes simultaneously oppressive and ex-
alting. As with the Kierkegaardian "rehearsal," it is in consenting to his own annihilation that man participates thus in
the universal Being.

Grenier had explained to Camus that alternation between
abandon and contraction that is the very life of the consciousness, a "systole" that turns it inward upon itself, a
block of revolt and denial followed by a "diastole" that
causes it to open itself to Nature in a bound of fervor and
forgetfulness verging on adoration. The religious experience that Grenier had learned from the Upanishads Camus
transposed to the level of a naturalistic "pantheism." In the
violence and contrasts of nature in Algeria, he saw the
symbol of those extreme states in which life is at the height
of its paroxysm. "Do not go there if you are only luke-
warm of heart [. . .] But for those who know the heartbreak of assent and refusal, of noon and midnights, of
revolt and love, for those, finally, who love bonfires beside
the sea, there is down there a flame that awaits them" (*Eté*,
p. 100). In the hell of Prague, Camus thought "desperately
of [his] city beside the sea, on summer evenings . . . very
gentle in the free light and full of young and beautiful
women." This is not only the nostalgic, sensual dream of
the *Méridional;* it is the orientation of a soul, a primordial
instinct that constrains Martha, in *Le Malentendu* (*Cross-
purposes*), to kill in order to be able finally to depart one
day for the land of sunlight. Such an attraction is mystical
because it is aroused by a being's need to grow inwardly. In
the presence of the desert that she sees for the first time,

even poor Janine, the heroine of *La Femme Adultère*,* a mediocre and banal person, knows a mysterious happiness: "She breathed deeply, she forgot the cold, the oppressiveness of other beings, the life of frenzy or stagnation, the long anguish of living and dying. After so many years of fleeing before fear, years of running wildly and aimlessly, she stopped at last. At the same time, she seemed to find her roots again, the sap rose anew in her body, which had quit trembling" (*ER*, p. 1572). Is this not to accede to another life, to true life? And does not Janine beneath the starlit sky undergo an authentically religious experience? "*In magnificentia naturae resurgit spiritus*" reads the pediment of a villa in Vicenza (*EE*, p. 98), a phrase that the entire Bible confirms. With Janine's ecstasy in mind, one thinks again of Dostoevski, of Alyosha's ambiguous yet so purely religious ecstasy, more of the Old Testament than Christian, that leads us to the very sources of religious sentiment: "The vault of heaven, full of soft shining stars, stretches vast and fathomless above him . . . The fresh, motionless, still night enfolded the earth . . . Alyosha stood, gazed, and suddenly threw himself down on the earth. He did not know why he embraced it. He could not have told why he longed so irresistibly to kiss it, to kiss it all. But he kissed it weeping . . ."** J. C. Brisville once put the following question to Camus: "You have written: 'The secret of my universe: to conceive of God without immortality of the soul.' Can you clarify your thinking on that point?" Here is Camus's response: "I have a sense of the sacred and I don't believe in a future life; that's all there is to it."***

---

* *Exil et le royaume* in *Théâtre, Récits, Nouvelles*, pp. 1555–73.

** Fëdor Dostoevski, *The Brothers Karamazov*, trans. Constance Garnett (New York, 1950), p. 436.

*** Jean-Claude Brisville, *Camus* (Paris, 1959), p. 260.

Yes, Camus had a sense of the *tremendum*, what the Greeks called *thambos*, the sentiment of primal mystery, the intuition that things are more than themselves and that a living presence is revealed through them. This is an instinct that survives all forms of revolt, all the successive contortions that mask the continuity of a fundamental assent. Here is a view of Florence as seen from San Miniato: "One of the only places in Europe where I understood that at the heart of my revolt a consent lay sleeping." A meditation upon the sensual world was necessary for that torn consciousness to become reunited with itself, to come full circle, to find its unity. There is thus within things a mysterious invitation to believe in happiness, to participate in some unity. An almost Plotinian ecstasy: "What is so strange about finding that union Plotinus wished for on earth? Unity is expressed here in terms of sun and sea" (*N*, p. 66), and further on: "At that minute, like the neophyte casting off his last veils, he abandons before his god the small change of his personality" (*N*, p. 94). An initiation preceded by detachment and followed by ecstasy, what Janine experiences face to face with the immense nocturnal horizon "where the sky and the earth joined in a pure line . . . Out there, it suddenly seemed to her, something was waiting for her which she had not known of until this day but which she had never ceased to miss . . . a knot tightened by the years, habit, and boredom slowly loosened . . . It seemed to her that the world's course had stopped just then and that from that instant on no one would grow old or die. Henceforth life was suspended everywhere except in her heart, within which, at that very moment, someone wept out of pain and awe" (*ER*, p. 1568).

This story is the first in a collection whose original title was *Nouvelles de l'Exil*—"News from Exile." Obedient to the principles of Camusian humanism, Janine, after a fleeting encounter with the Immense, returns courageously to take her place in the midst of human mediocrity. For, such a meeting with the Immense is an act of infidelity to the human compact and merits the name of adultery. Camus's response to the mysterious appeal that came to him from Nature was never without a touch of bad conscience. Thus the night, the sea, the deserts, the absence of men—all put him in an indecisive state of mind in which sadness and the feeling of plenitude were mixed, a state in which poetic revery touched upon religious emotion. Camus, in the presence of physical immensity, discovered an intimate immensity whose earthly horizons are like a projection or a symbol. For an instant, man thought he was becoming a god, that he was becoming one with God, while at the same time the distance that separates him from that fullness drives him to the verge of tears. Camus knew that he could not cross that distance. The torture and the delight of Tantalus: he will not make the liberating gesture; he will remain trembling with admiration and nostalgia on the threshold of a temple that his reason obliges him to believe uninhabited. The sacred becomes blurred and soon nothing remains but the "world's tender indifference."

But that admiration and nostalgia were enough to change everything. Sartre did not experience them, certainly; his first reaction in the presence of objective reality was one of revulsion, indeed, one of disgust. But nausea is no longer possible when one has begun by admiring; despair is not the same in a consciousness that has held, if only for an instant, the sentiment of beauty. Camus was one of those who ingenuously consented to admire and that was enough to give his humanism an entirely different scope. What is lacking in the modern world, he wrote in 1948, is "nature, the sea, hillsides, meditation at evening-time" (*Eté*, p. 110).

Such phrases, their "romanticism" and their estheticism, are easily ridiculed. In fact, however, Camus is touching an open wound. Men of our time, enclosed in their large cities, have consecrated themselves to what they call History because they live only in the streets; they are imprisoned in their own citadels. They are separated from what precedes History (Nature) and from what is above and beyond it (Beauty). Isolated in a universe that has become foreign to them in the process of their own profaning of it, they are bent on constructing "the world of man." They no longer experience nostalgia for that other world, their "true homeland" (*Eté*, p. 84), which may be glimpsed in the splendor of the star-filled sky or of the sunlight on the sea. Thus men have lost contact with the infinite and have themselves shrunk to the proportions of their earthly projects. "Only one Provençal evening, one perfect hill, a trace of salt in the air is all that is needed to see that everything is still to do" (*Eté*, p. 84)—an unusual remark, even an absurd one for anyone who has not experienced the purifying virtue of admiration. Yes, everything is still to be done. That is to say that nothing will ever be done, that nothing human has any real value, that History is perhaps only a mirage compared to these sensual fulfillments. Caligula at the extreme limit his nihilism attains has only one interlocutor worthy of him, the young Scipion who, however, hates him and whose father has been put to death by Caligula. For if Caligula embodies the absolute of refusal, scorn, and despair, Scipion is, like Kirillov, Versilov, or Alyosha—like Camus himself—in communion with the all mysterious beauty of the universe. Caligula has passed over to the other side, he is "pure in evil" as Scipion is "pure in goodness." The latter speaks "of a certain *harmony* between the earth and the foot . . . and also of the line of Roman hills and of that

fugitive overpowering peace that evening brings to them
. . . and of that subtle minute where the sky still filled with
gold suddenly overturns and shows us in an instant its other
face, overflowing with shining stars . . . etc" (CL, p. 57).
Caligula, Scipion—a strange dialogue involving two ages of
life, two diametrically opposite experiences. The one is still
completely filled with adolescent awe and everything for
him "assumes the face of love"; the other has encountered
death and men's sufferings: he is a Scipion grown older, one
whose disappointment nothing can assuage and who takes
his revenge for what he has seen by multiplying the evil
around him. Just as Alyosha and Ivan Karamazov represent
facets of Dostoevski, Caligula and Scipion embody the twin
faces of reality as Camus saw them. He declared, speaking
to a journalist in 1951: "I did not begin my life by way of
heartbreak. In the same way, I did not come to be a writer
by the way of imprecation or disparagement as many have,
but by way of admiration" (PL/II, p. 1338). On the worst
of days, his resentment against other beings and things
dissolved anew in the presence of "the evening's promise"
and in that of the "signs of summer skies." There were
always within him—and even within Clamence in *La
Chute*—those escapes into the fresh air, far from the stone
cities, symbols of human encirclement.

Equivocal experiences from which Camus drew an
equivocal lesson. Rapture in the beauty of the world only
served finally to strengthen the fervor of his attachment to
the earth. "Shall I ask myself if something is dying and if
men are suffering when everything is written in that window where the sky pours down its fullness to encounter
my pity?" (EE, p. 123). All anguish, like all despair, is put
between parentheses: "I am gratified before having desired.

Eternity is there and I was hoping for it"—"Live *as if*," he writes again; "in spite of much searching, therein lies all my knowledge" (*EE*, p. 125). To live by imitating things, to share their serenity, to forget evil and death in that "opaque intoxication which the sun pours forth" (*ET*, p. 1165),* to act "as if" the *sun, kisses and wild aromas* filled all the needs of our soul, in short, occupy the earth in the manner of the god Pan and commune thus with the universal; such was Camus's abiding temptation. If this temptation held sway mainly during his adolescence, it accompanied him all his life like a wondrous and dangerous mirage. Resistant to the alternate temptation of pity and despair, he wished to make of this world his Kingdom while closing his eyes to men's misfortune and exhausting all the pleasures life offered him: "To clasp a woman's body, is also to hold against oneself that strange joy which descends from the sun toward the sea" (*N*, p. 20). Thus the hierodules, the sacred prostitutes, offered themselves at the doors of the temples of Asia; physical love puts us in touch with beneficent forces; it is grafted on to universal life. They were "terrestrial," Camus's gods—they became identical with love of life in a man entirely gratified by the gifts of nature. Here, then, is Camus's "religion": an intense and, one might say, divine joy in living and in feeling. In effect, this amounts to saying that he was given the capacity for finding his paradise if only the sky were blue and the Mediterranean on the horizon. In this he was like the ancient Greeks of whom he said, in his thesis for the *Diplôme*

---

* M. Onimus offers this phrase from *L'Etranger* as a direct quotation: "ivresse opaque que déverse le soleil." Actually it is a paraphrase of the original text, which reads: ". . . triompher du soleil et de cette ivresse opaque qu'il me déversait" (*ET*, p. 1165) [trans. note].

d'Etudes supérieures (1936), that they "accepted a sportive and esthetic justification for their existence. The outline of their hills or a young man running along a beach revealed to them the world's entire secret. Their gospel said: our Kingdom is of this world."* Such was Camus's gospel during his entire lifetime—taking into account certain variations of which we will speak later—the same gospel that resurfaced in so surprising and spontaneous a manner in 1951 in the final pages of *L'Homme révolté* (*The Rebel*). One must never forget that the "philosopher of the Absurd" was before everything else a happy man who saw himself bound to a harmonious whole through admiration, love, and—sometimes—rapture.

The Exile

"Everywhere a thin film of sunlight that would split under one's nail but which clothes all things with an eternal smile" (*EE*, p. 122).

A thin film of sunlight . . . No! Light and beauty do not suffice to "fill up the fissures of the soul." Such ecstasies rarely last; the impression of plenitude is replaced, alas, with the spectacle of reality. Daily experience resembles that coin picked up on the beach at Tipasa (*Eté*, p. 153): on one side a beautiful face of a woman and on the other "a corroded face" that feels all rough beneath one's fingers.

At the age of seventeen, in his "philosophy year,"** the young Camus discovered that *corroded face* which the young Algérois' adolescent ingenuousness had hidden from

* *Métaphysique chrétienne et néoplatonisme* in *Essais* (Paris: Edition de la Pléiade, 1965), p. 1225.

** The *classe de philosophie* of the French *lycée* is the last year of study preceding presentation for the baccalaureate examination [trans. note].

him until then. Philosophical reflection, the experience of illness, the spectacle of injustice in a colonial land made him aware of suffering, of old age, of social hypocrisy, and of death; henceforth the world would have for him two faces: the "right" side and the "wrong."* An anguish would be born out of the immense contrast between overflowing harmony and disorder that had become evident.

The *Carnets* (*Notebooks*) from 1936 are filled with these oppositions in black and white—pages of lyrical fervor are intermingled with bitter and cruel observations—two styles, almost two forms of music. Sometimes, strangely, the two sentiments blend and produce that ambiguous tone so characteristic of Camus: "And even amid that sadness within me, what desire to love and what intoxication at the mere sight of a hillside in the evening air" (*CN*, p. 38). One thinks of the last pages of *La Peste* (*The Plague*), written seven years later. Rieux has just learned of his wife's death: "He held the open telegram . . . and stubbornly contemplated through the window a magnificent morning that was dawning over the sea" (*LP*, p. 1458) . . . Stubbornly, as if to blind himself with sunlight and silence his protest. But everywhere, in the very brilliance of the sunlight (the sunlight of Africa speaks of death), Camus discovered that double aspect of things. Like Barrès, like D'Annunzio,** like his masters and an-

* The "right" and "wrong" sides are a reference to Camus's early collection of essays, *L'Envers et l'endroit*, (*The Right Side and the Wrong Side*), first published in Algiers in 1938 [trans. note].

** Maurice Barrès (1862–1923), French writer whose works, especially *Le Culte du Moi* and *Les Déracinés*, had a great influence on French youth of the 1920's and 1930's.

Gabriele D'Annunzio (1863–1938), the Italian novelist, dramatist, and poet, had a large following in France (where he resided from 1910–1915) during the first third of the twentieth

cestors, the Spanish writers, he sensed the close proximity
of decay and of brilliance. But what with so many others
was only a pretext for effects, he dramatically lived. He
strove to be on both sides at once and "to accept with an
equal force the yes and the no" (CN, p. 38). For a long
time, he believed himself able, in fact, to sustain the *yes*
even while vaguely sensing its fragility. "Without being a
dupe I chose appearances . . . A balance was taking form,
colored however by the full apprehension of its own end"
(EE, p. 112). A moment came, between 1936 and 1938,
when the face of Medusa definitely seemed to carry the
day. The evidence of evil then effaced all but the memory
of harmony and of the Kingdom. Henceforth the word
exile reappears beneath his pen: *Le Malentendu* was to
have been called *L'Exilé: La Peste, Les Exilés* and, beginning with his first essays, we see him preoccupied with
death, evil, hope; a heavy sadness penetrates the most lyrical passages of *Noces*, of *L'Eté*. Soon the landscapes become rarer, the descriptions drier. He finds brief allusions
sufficient (*Caligula, La Peste*, etc.). Nature appears only
sporadically in the form of dazzling "flashbacks." As the
world of men invades his thought, landscapes fade. It might
be said that in humanizing himself he learned to be unhappy: "To the extent that I separate myself from the
world I come to fear death, to the extent that I become
attached to the fate of men who are living, instead of
contemplating the sky that endures" (N, p. 41). Camus's
merit lies in his having finally chosen—unlike so many
oriental mystics—that fear in order to become attached "to

---

century. See Giovanni Gullace, *Gabriele D'Annunzio in
France* (Syracuse: University of Syracuse Press, 1966) [trans.
note].

the fate of men who are living," at the risk of breaking the spell of his innocence and his happiness.

"Everything begins with consciousness and only through it does anything become worthwhile," one reads in *Le Mythe de Sisyphe* (*MS*, p. 27). But ten pages earlier the author had acknowledged: "to begin to think is to be consumed . . . The worm resides in the heart of man." Such is the paradox of the human condition: the awaking of lucidity coincides with distaste for life. To be happy must one not remain blind? Unhappiness is, first of all, of an intellectual order; then it afflicts the vital forces of the soul and withers everything right up to the heart. Like his hero, Caligula, Camus lived the tragedy of the intellect.

Jean Grenier brought to his pupils the living example of a thinker who is fundamentally Christian but, suffering from this "metaphysical sickness," is tormented by contingency and in search of a serenity that Grenier sought, for his part, in the unconsciousness of the cat, Mouloud,* or in the mystical emptiness of yoga. To his pupils Grenier undoubtedly rendered the greatest service a professor of philosophy can render: he *disturbed* them. Few books are more disturbing, indeed, than his collection of essays, *Les Iles* (*The Isles*), first published in 1933. Through meditation upon obscure myths, the author attempts to transmit a certain anguish. "I owe to Grenier a sense of *doubt* that will never end and that has prevented me, for example, from being a humanist in the sense that it is understood today, I mean a man blinded by brief certainties" (Preface to *Les Iles*, p. 12). Without Grenier, Camus lacked that

---

* Mouloud was the name of Jean Grenier's cat, to which he devotes considerable discussion in *Les Iles* (Paris: Gallimard, 1959), pp. 33–64; he uses the cat as an example of a living creature in harmony with the natural world [trans. note].

dimension of *doubt* that opens humanism to transcendence and renders it dissatisfied. In short, Grenier shattered the "film of sunlight"; he revealed another mystery (or another sacred object), no longer the entirely external one of light, but that of shadows. Grenier is a philosopher of *emptiness;* he underwent his crucial experience one day at the foot of a tree, and here is what he saw: "Stretched out in the shade of a linden, contemplating an almost cloudless sky, I saw that sky *topple and become engulfed in the void.*"* Camus until that moment had felt almost the opposite. When one has undergone such an experience of the illusory character of appearances, one is seized by an immense anger, the need to jostle all those façades. "An internal anger against the miserable role that men are destined to play and that they take so seriously . . . hence the desire to shock . . . ,"** and already Grenier thought of the strange figure of Caligula. Camus followed with passion this logic, which he would later find in Ivan Karamazov and Stavrogin; a universe of ideas and of feelings was opening up for him.

That Mediterranean soul, made for a happy and limited wisdom, was drawn by a mind come from a northern land toward a vision of things in which Being seemed to become all the more dim as one penetrated the more deeply into the truth. Henceforth, the dialogue—an endless dialogue—was not between the world and man, but within man. The gods of happiness are themselves circumscribed. Doubt and its vertigo infected Camus with a virus of which he was never to be cured.

This sense of transcendence Camus soon discovered in

* *Les Iles,* p. 25.
** *Les Iles,* p. 76.

Melville. The voyage of Captain Ahab in quest of the white whale is once more Grenier's metaphysical voyage from isle to isle with the addition of final frustration and the revelation of the Absurd. Moby Dick! "One of the most staggering myths that anyone has ever imagined surrounding man's combat against evil and the irresistible logic that in the end pits the just man against creation and the creator to begin with, then against his fellowman and against himself."* This book did more than "stagger" Camus. It established for the first time a relation between the divine and the monstrous, between evil and the creator, between the passion for the Absolute and Revolt. This book, essentially religious and completely impregnated with the Bible, was understood by Camus as a cry of anger, a "Promethean myth." Ahab's defeat was not in his eyes the punishment of an excess but an appeal to further violence; the Absolute must be destroyed because it is itself the destroyer of man. Camus was to spend the rest of his life killing the White Whale all over again.

The hold over Camus of the pessimistic André Malraux of 1930 was deep. In *La Tentation de l'occident* (*The Temptation of the West*), published in 1926, Camus read that "at the center of European man, dominating the broad movements of his life, is an essential absurdity" and that "thought, becoming an object unto itself, attacks the world much more than passion." Of Malraux's most somber book, *Le Temps du mépris* (The Time of Derision) he said: "I loved that book."

* Preface to *Moby Dick* (Paris: Gallimard, 1955). I have not had the opportunity of seeing this preface; however, what appears to be the same essay appears in *PL/II*, pp. 1899–1903; see also *Lyrical and Critical Essays* (Knopf, 1968) [trans. note].

In Tolstoi, on the other hand, he came upon the terror of the soul and religious nostalgia in its native, almost morbid, state: "There is in Tolstoi an anguish, a sense of the tragic doubtlessly less spectacular than one finds in Dostoevski, but which I continue to find overwhelming because it was his lot right up to the end" (*PL/II*, p. 1339).* Camus found other examples of this anguish, of course, but in more literary and composed form in Dostoevski. What is astonishing is that this happy and very unpuritanical Algérois should have consorted with such writers, that he should have been sensitive to such an extent to the Slavic experience of guilt and universal evil . . . These writers touched Camus on a level beyond social indignation, beyond political or even philosophical ideology, at the point, indeed, where only the terms of despair or salvation can have any meaning. An atmosphere of sadness impregnates his first essays; in the midst of images of happiness a hideous face surges up repeatedly, like the music-hall performer he saw in Palma surrounded by joy but with despair in the depths of her empty eyes (*EE*, p. 108). Camus did not accept a destiny in which one could not possess life in its fullness; like Anouilh's Antigone he wants "everything and right now." We shall see how, after the war, his humanism was to become less demanding, how he would even come to loathe this passion for the absolute. But in his youth Camus rebelled against old age, suffering, mediocrity, death, and atrocious universal contingency—against "the absence of

---

* M. Onimus lists the source of this quotation as "*Nouvelles littéraires*, 1943." It is actually found in an interview Camus granted to Gabriel d'Aubarède, "Rencontre avec Albert Camus," *Nouvelles littéraires*, No. 1236 (May 10, 1951), pp. 1 and 6. The article is reprinted in the Pléiade edition of *Essais*, pp. 1337–43 [trans. note].

any deep reason for living, the senselessness of that frenzy
of everyday activity and the uselessness of suffering" (*MS*,
p. 18).

Camus's experience resembled that of Buddha when he
left the paradise of his childhood. It could have led him to
the same conclusions . . .

The meeting with misery: life in Belcourt,* the filthy
staircase, the ugliness of the apartment: "the rot and the
bareness of three-rooms-and-kitchen," writes a witness, "the
cries (and even the shrieks), the icy tile floors for it is very
cold in Algiers in the winter, the laundry in the windows,
the odors of garlic, of fish, of urine."** Yes, Camus
henceforth saw these things—and also the torpor, the bru-
talization they produced, the silent resignation. "Who
taught you all that?" Tarrou asks and Rieux's response is
immediate: "Misery" (*LP*, p. 1322). Camus began to hear
and listen. Rare are those who dare heed misery for what it
reveals, destroys with swift sureness every possibility of
self-centered happiness. A book lent him by Grenier made
Camus attentive to it; at sixteen he read a moving work by
André de Richaud, *La Douleur:* "He painted poor milieux,
he described nostalgias that I had experienced . . ." (*PL/II*,
p. 1338).*** Some years later, the miserable poverty he

---

* Belcourt was a poor quarter of Algiers inhabited by work-
ing class Europeans and Arabs; after his father's death in 1914,
Camus lived here with his family until his entry into the
Université d'Alger in 1933 [trans. note].

** Anne Durand, *Le Cas Albert Camus* (Paris [1961]), p.
19.

*** M. Onimus gives the source of this remark as "*Nouvelles
littéraires*, nov. 1945." It is, however, from a 1951 interview
published in that review and reprinted in the Pléiade edition of
Essais (see note, p. 52) [trans. note].

met in Kabylia* deprived him "of the right to enjoy the beauty of the world" (*A III*, p. 909). Like Péguy, like so many other sincere and generous souls—in experiencing misery Camus entered into the profoundness of life.

He encountered old age: his grandmother, immobile and silent, whom life was slowly deserting, whom the young people abandoned in the evening to go to the movies while she stayed behind seated in her chair, her rosary in her hand —an old woman "whom no one listens to anymore, a death that compensates for nothing, and then, on the other side of the scale, the world's brilliance" (*EE*, p. 54). Everywhere derision, everywhere scandal . . . The child went away, heavy-hearted, leaving the old woman to her solitude. But he had discovered the pitiless cruelty of life: "to do one's duty and accept being a man leads only to *being old*" (*EE*, p. 67).

And then he encountered illness. At the age of fifteen, at the *lycée* in the midst of his intellectual development, he fell sick. At seventeen he was informed off-handedly that he was tubercular. A glance at the *Carnets* is enough to measure his sense of shock. That experience separated him physically from happiness as "metaphysical concern" had separated him from appearances. "When the body is sorrowful," Clamence says, "the heart languishes . . . Yes, I think certainly that it was then that everything began"

* Kabylia, in the mountains east of Algiers, is inhabited by Berbers whose principal occupation is farming. Kabylia was struck by a devastating famine in 1937–1938. Camus, then a reporter for the daily *Alger-Républicain*, visited the region and wrote a series of eleven articles on conditions there and on steps the government might take to alleviate them. Some of these articles are reprinted in *Actuelles III*. For a brief discussion of these articles, see Emmett Parker, *Albert Camus: The Artist in the Arena* (Madison: University of Wisconsin Press, 1965), pp. 31–36 [trans. note].

(*LC*, p. 1495). "Everything," that is to say, lucidity and revolt against the lie of happiness.

This was also the moment Camus encountered death. He was obsessed with it throughout those years and that contemplation produced in him "the giddiness of those who have looked too long into a bottomless crevice." Camus was afraid with an entirely physical fear—in no way religious —the fear of annihilation. But the thought of death, far from driving him toward promises of immortality, turned him passionately toward life. In order to conquer Medusa, Camus chose then to stare her down, to imbue himself with "the conscious certainty of a death without hope . . . Youth must be that, this hard *tête-à-tête* with death" (*N*, p. 39). He attempted to rediscover the serenity and the discretion of men of former times, "the innocence of the ancients confronted with their destiny." "The only freedom possible is a freedom with regard to death. The truly free man is he who, accepting death for what it is, at the same time accepts its consequences" (*CN*, p. 148). Epictetus joins with Kirillov in order to help Camus harden his gaze and to free himself of anguish. *Le Mythe de Sisyphe* was structured on the idea of suicide as a liberation accepted as the parting hypothesis. But nothing does any good; Camus is too sincere—too attached to the Kingdom —not to tell of his trembling. "I do not want to lie or to have anyone lie to me; I want to bear my lucidity the entire distance and to look straight at my final end *with the total profusion of my jealousy and my horror*" (*N*, p. 41). The terrible jealousy of the dying man, the condemned man in the presence of those who will survive him: "To be there with his entire life in his hands, all his fear deep in his guts, and a stupid stare . . ." (*N*, p. 41). Camus lived this nightmare at the time of his illness; his work as a writer would permit him to relive it with a strange pleasure. One of his first projects, apparently inspired by Dostoevski, was to write the journal of a condemned man (*CN*, pp. 24 and 29), which would come to fruition in the final passages of *L'Etranger*. His mother had described to him the shocked face and the silence of his father who had gone to attend an execution at Constantine. Camus's reflections on the guillotine, marked by such revolting realism, are well known, as are his campaigns against capital punishment. In truth, Camus never ceased to tremble at the thought of death; his work is thoroughly overcast with it. It reigns in his first essays, it triumphs in *La Peste*, and it is the "discovery" of death that renders Caligula lucid. Fundamentally, for Camus, all men—even the most believing—are convinced that death is final (even if they pretend to believe in another life). It is indeed this common knowledge that sets men apart and should seal their union. The basis of their fraternity is formed of terror.

Travel, far from distracting Camus, aggravated his sense of fragility. There is a little of death in every separation: "What gives travel value, is fear . . ." (*CN*, p. 26). Far from home one is less protected against anguish; the curtain of habit, the comfortable fabric of gestures and words where the heart found its ease is slowly lifted and reveals finally the pale face of inquietude: "Man is face to face with himself; I defy him to be happy" (*EE*, p. 88). In Camus there is an ontology of the traveler; he assents to the stripping away of habit and routine. Camus went seeking, in travel, not a diversion but a truth. Such is the "restive happiness" that Mersault experiences at the end of his voyage in *La Mort heureuse*. Still again, to gain self-insight Clamence will leave his country and his friends. Is not a traveler always more or less a soul in trouble, a symbol of lost and wandering humanity?

A few sparse entries in the *Carnets* seem to show that Camus's youthful experience of love was a disenchantment. Beyond question, he did happen to say that no certainty was worth "a hair of a woman's head" (*ET*, p. 1208). But this was said in a thesis novel,* therefore, a not impartial one, of which we will speak later. Certainly it was easy for a rich and overflowing sensuality to unfold in that city "without complexes," where enjoyment displayed itself ingenuously in the sunlight. But here again, Camus is too demanding for mere "tourism" to satisfy him. He never possessed anything of love except the gestures and the semblances; never did the Kingdom seem so near and never was exile more clearly felt. "At a certain moment one can no longer experience the emotion of love. There remains only the tragic" (*CN*, p. 246). And what is the tragic if not the sentiment of finitude, of satiety, or of death. In going through this experience Caligula becomes mad. "To love, nothing is less sure. One can know what the suffering of love is; one does not know what love is. Here it is privation, regret, empty hands. I shall not know its joyful ardor, for me there remains only its anguish. *A hell where everyone expects Paradise*. It is a hell none the less" (*CN*, p. 228). Thus love is defined negatively, by way of what destroys or obstructs it, and that light, without which life would be only shadows, vanishes as soon as one catches sight of it. Love occupies a minor place in Camus's work—perhaps out of a sense of modesty but also out of lucidity. If Rieux, if Rambert are in love, it is no doubt because they are

---

* The *roman à thèse* or "thesis novel" in French is generally taken to be a novel that sets out to prove or to convince the reader of the validity of a certain hypothesis of the author. That this definition could be made to apply to *L'Etranger* is debatable [trans. note].

painfully separated from their loved ones. In *Caligula*, Scipion, symbol of tenderness and youth, has not yet left the Kingdom. This youth who knows no exile also does not know love; he has only attained its state of "cosmic" ecstasy. And in the same play the sad and pitiful Caesonia incarnates the devotion of the wife; Caligula is pleased to scoff at her before all and sundry and ends by killing her. "Teach us the indifference that allows love to be born over and over again," he says bitterly, and it is from indifference, in fact, that the Don Juanism is born that Camus praises in *Le Mythe de Sisyphe:* the man who compensates quality with quantity. "Why must one love rarely in order to love a great deal?" (*MS*, p. 97). Alas! What a disappointment! To love often is not to love at all. Ten years later Clamence straightforwardly admits this truth: "I loved them all . . . which comes down to saying I never loved any one of them . . . authentic love is exceptional: about two or three cases in a century. The rest of the time it is vanity or boredom" (*LC*, p. 1502). By what mystery do we know what authentic love is, if it is indeed true that we never experience it. Is not love the tangible and daily proof of exile? . . .

The two simultaneous experiences of the Kingdom and of Exile opened within Camus an interior space that is the domain of "metaphysical concern." It is also the domain of religions. Before explaining Camus's attempts to rid himself of a "burden of concern" that he sometimes considered a personal infirmity or a failing of his epoch, we must explain why he always so consistently* refused the solutions and courses of action that religion offered him.

* And so explicitly [trans. note].

2

No to God

A natural sense of the sacred, a lucidity that pierced through appearances to the light beyond, a soul aware of its exile and in quest of certainties and reasons to live—are not all the elements present that usually form a religious awareness? Why did Camus from the first, and continuously thereafter, reject the enticement of Christianity? Since his position on this point was essentially undeviating, we will examine it in this chapter without taking into account any evolution—which, moreover, is not discernible from presently available documents. One must carefully scrutinize the texts to discover any sign of a rapprochement between Camus and Christianity after 1944. If it happened that, in 1948, he appealed to the Christians in order to broaden the struggle against absolutisms and the Marxist ideology and so that they might participate in the defense of "man," his complementary distrust toward Christian absolutism remained equally keen. On the level of principles, the divergence is complete. Of what does it consist?

But, first, what knowledge and what experience of Christianity did Camus actually have?

He was baptized. Baptism, first communion, marriage—
rites to which people accord respect. But his religious in-
struction was almost nonexistent. For two years he at-
tended the Thursday morning catechism classes at his parish in Belcourt. In the spring of 1923, when he was ten, his
grandmother, who was anxious to have him make his first
communion, insisted to the parish priest that it take place
earlier than was customary so that in the following year he
would not be "distracted from his studies." Contrary to
what he sometimes said, then, Camus was not raised entirely outside Christianity, but what he knew of it and the
experiences that he had had of it on the threshold of adolescence amounted to very little. Religion made up of absurd
superstitions, designed to reassure, to console the sick and
the aged such as his grandmother.* Religion petrified by
habit, without true faith or true love, the mania of the old, a
kind of pitiful bauble. And Camus's mother, that mother to
whom he would remain so tenderly attached all his life, and

* M. Onimus errs in attributing the following episode
from *L'Envers et l'endroit* (see also "An Old People's Religion," p. 135) to an occurrence in Camus's own family. The
"old woman" in this sketch was not modeled after Camus's
own grandmother, Marie Sintès, nor is the "daughter" referred
to in this passage Camus's mother. Quilliot points out in a note
to his commentaries on *L'Envers et l'endroit* that "according
to M. Lucien Camus [Camus's older brother], it was while
acting as a tutor to a little girl that Camus came to know the
old woman with the lead crucifix, her grandmother" (*PL/II*, p.
1176). Moreover, one has only to compare the sketch of Marie
Sintès in the third section of the same essay (*PL/II*, pp. 20–22),
to see at once that Camus's grandmother was a woman of quite
different stamp from the one presented here. In point of fact,
M. Onimus's analysis of Camus's family's role in his religious
formation is based on the sketchiest of biographical documentation [trans. note].

who provided him the model for a silent, ingenuously stoic and as though impenetrable humanism. She had long since ceased to practice her faith and made light of her old mother's paternosters: " 'There she is praying again!' 'What is it to you?' the sick woman used to reply, 'It's nothing to me, but it finally gets on my nerves . . .' And the old woman fell silent fixing on her daughter a long stare filled with reproaches" (*EE*, p. 39). One can envision the scene. And one can also see the child who listens and wonders: the dialogue of two women who represent two generations and two times of life. "The old woman would add: 'She'll see, she will, when she's old. She too will need them!' " Religion comes then with the medicine bottles, at the age when what is vital flees or becomes numb. Thus God is part and parcel with wrinkles, loneliness, and immobility; He replaces life. But let life return and God no longer has any weight. In Algeria, Camus as child did not meet God among the living but in the darkness, beside the dying. His mother, a widow with two children, had by her efforts alone to shelter, to clothe, and to feed four people. She did housework in the morning and in the evening, when she came home, more work awaited her. Poverty wore out her sensitivity and, so to speak, petrified her. There is in Algeria, moreover, a hardness that Camus took for solidity, a destitution that he took for simplicity, an aridity in which he saw purity. On the basis of this prosaic consciousness, on this rock of indifference and coldness the child, become an adolescent, was to construct his spiritual life. Camus always mistrusted the religious emotion because he learned to place above everything the lucidity of a positive spirit, whether it be cynical or nihilist. He was to say many times that one could not "imagine God"—which appeared to him to be an argument in favor of His nonexistence; but by this verb he designates a sentiment much more than an image. Closed off from childhood to prayer, to the summoning up of the invisible, he would not later experience the person of God except under the aspect of an absence and a lack, of a hollowness or a vacuum. When he did portray a priest (Paneloux in *La Peste*), he showed us a prepossessed or tortured intelligence, but not a sensitivity. Camus never envisioned religion except from without.

The importance of these early adolescent experiences cannot be exaggerated; Camus was neither psychologically nor morally prepared to transcend the evidence and the obstacle of that lucidity which is like an intellectual transposition of the virtues and the faults of his mother. God could never be for him anything but an idea, a word, that is to say, a habit. "Do you believe in God?" Rieux is asked in *La Peste*. The response is clear enough but odd: "No. But what does that mean?" (*LP*, p. 1320); and we remember that Meursault sums up thus his position before the chaplain who had come to see him in prison where he awaited death: "I was perhaps not sure of what truly interested me, but I was entirely sure of what did not interest me" (*ET*, p. 1205). This must not be seen as any kind of provocation; it is the prosaic pronouncement of a fact. Meursault embodies the agnostic positivism that Camus lived in the presence of his mother and his comrades. Immediate realities, the pleasure and the hardships of existence seemed to them a much more important matter, and God remained exiled from them in the irreal. How would this boy know, unless by a miracle, the lifting of the heart that carries all else with it, and which has been so well evoked by, for example, a Claudel:

"*I am indeed the son of woman! for how true it is that reason and the lessons of masters and of absurdity, all of these have not any hold*

"Against the upheaval of my heart and against the out-held hands of this little child.

"Oh tears, oh too feeble heart, oh well of tears that surges.

*"Come ye faithful and let us adore this newborn child."**

This brief citation opens on to another world. Camus could only remain faithful to "reason" and to the "lesson of the masters" because no well of tears ever surged in his heart. Cosmic ecstasy, that is ecstasy which is at once sensual and cerebral in conjunction with metaphysical concern, is not enough to render a soul Christian! It is enough to create a malaise, a need, but it will forever lack the impulse of tenderness, that impetuosity that brings illumination.

To these negative influences must be added the Voltairian remarks of his uncle, M. Acault, a self-taught butcher who had put at Camus's disposal a disparate library where Gide sat next to the eighteenth-century *philosophes*. The consequences of anticlericalism in the formation of a youthful sensitivity must not be ignored; antipathy for its ministers strikes at religion itself. A scholarship student in a bourgeois *lycée* (oh, how many like him!),** he saw Catholicism torn apart in Metropolitan France by the then recent condemnation of the *Action Française*** exhibiting before

---

* Paul Claudel, "Cinq grandes Odes," *Œuvres complètes*, I (Paris, 1950), p. 94.

** The *lycée*—and the state-operated French school system in general—have commonly been considered, with some justification, by French Catholics as militantly anticlerical [trans. note].

*** *L'Action française* was an extreme right-wing political review holding royalist and fascist views; it advocated "integral nationalism." It was founded in 1899 by Charles Maurras (1868–1952), its leading political theorist. In 1926 the Holy See

the world its extreme right roots and the conservative tend-
encies of its hierarchy. Everything combined to separate
him from a religion professed by the moneyed class and
practiced in fact by women and old men. When he read
Zarathustra in 1937, Camus could have taken Nietzsche's
apostrophes for his own without hesitation. One is not
astonished, then, that breaking with the traditions of his
upbringing, he contracted a civil marriage in 1933. In fact,
he lived all those formative years totally in the margins of
Christianity: "I do not part from the principle that the
Christian truth is illusory," he was to say in 1946 to the
Dominicans of Latour-Maubourg. "I never entered into
it, that is all."* Jean Guitton's book on M. Pouget,
published in 1943, which Camus's sympathy for Guitton
—whose dissertation had inspired his thesis—and the forced
idleness of the Occupation led him to read, was for him a
revelation. He found there the portrait of a priest, open,
intelligent, with a very lucid critical mind accompanied by
a profound piety. That reading struck him. The article that

---

placed certain of Maurras' books and the *Action française* itself
on the Index, seriously diluting thereby much of its effective-
ness among French clergy and loyal Catholics [trans. note].

* The speech to the Dominicans of the Latour-Maubourg
monastery took place in 1946, not in 1948 as indicated in
Actuelles I (see *PL/II*, p. 1597). Camus's remarks from that
speech are contained in *Actuelles I* (Pléiade edition of *Essais*,
p. 371). The citation given by M. Onimus, who does not give a
source, differs somewhat from that in *Actuelles I*. Onimus
quotes the following, which I have translated: "Je ne pars pas
du principe que la vérité chrétienne est illusoire, dira-t-il en
1946 aux dominicains de la rue de Latour-Maubourg. Je n'y
suis jamais entré, voilà tout." *Actuelles I* reads: ". . . je ne
partirai jamais du principe que la vérité chrétienne est illusoire,
mais seulement de ce fait que je n'ai pu y entrer" [trans. note].

he published in the *Cahiers du sud* (April, 1943) gives the impression of a discovery.* "Ah!" he wrote in December to Guitton, "if the Catholic religion had been that of your M. Pouget!" One can see in these words the mark of a prejudice as well as of a regret.

We shall distinguish between Camus's attitude toward religion in general and toward Christianity as he thought he understood it.

Where religion is concerned it was a question of objections based on principles that, from the outset, channeled and rendered fruitless the intellectual approaches of which we will speak further on.

Camus, a fiercely independent free-thinker, could not bear to settle down anywhere, neither in a job nor in any one philosophy. In order to remain free he turned down a position as a teacher. In the same spirit he left the Communist Party, to which his sympathy for the Moslem poor of Algeria had attracted him. His break with Stalinist Marxism in 1945 had no other cause. Every totalitarian doctrine was odious to him because it alienated and mutilated. Jean Grenier had apparently communicated to him a scorn for the spirit of orthodoxy and a creed of free thought, the heritage of what was most precious in the Greek spirit, Socratism. "The Greeks did not deny the gods but they did allocate to them their share. Christianity, which is a total religion, cannot admit this attitude."** Such is the redhib-

* "Portrait d'un élu," *Les Cahiers du sud*, No. 225 (April, 1943), p. 306. Reprinted in the Pléiade edition of *Essais*, pp. 1597–1603 [trans. note].

** M. Onimus does not make clear whether he is citing a statement of Grenier or of Camus, nor does he indicate a source [trans. note].

itory defect: all religion is total that claims to deliver a definitive and eternal truth. And totalitarianism in all its forms is at the same time the destruction and the supreme temptation of the mind. It is so convenient to repeat a catechism and thus interrupt the questioning and the protest that are natural to a living consciousness! All the more dangerous in that while bringing promises of life its seduction is exercised on those who hunger and thirst for perenniality. Religion "dehumanizes" and weakens the forces of revolt: "If in the sacred world one does not find the problem of revolt, it is that in truth one does not find in it any real problematic questions, since all the answers are given at one fell swoop. Metaphysics is replaced by myth. There are no longer any interrogations; there are only answers and eternal commentaries . . . For a human mind there can be only two possible universes, that of the sacred (or in the language of Christianity, of grace) and that of revolt" (*HR*, p. 34). Thus, for Camus, the realm of the sacred or grace is a symbol of servitude.

When it happened—rarely—that Camus spoke of religion, it was nearly always to allude to religious wars, to fanaticism, to ecclesiastical politics. Catholicism in particular seemed to have betrayed Christ in coming to terms with the world and in founding an "empire." It was not in vain that Camus had read the legend of the Grand Inquisitor.* On several occasions he opposed Jesus thus to those who claimed to act in his name. "Pardon on their lips and condemnation in their hearts," they were never able to follow the example of forgiveness that He had set for them. "They have perched him up on a judge's seat in the secrecy

* See Fëdor Dostoevski, *The Brothers Karamazov*, trans. Constance Garnett (New York, 1950), pp. 292–313 [trans. note].

of their hearts and they strike hard; above all they judge, they judge in His name" (*LC*, p. 1532). There is thus an ineluctable intimacy between men of religion and tyrants, whatever their respective doctrines. One finds a striking example in the words of the Examining Magistrate brandishing a crucifix under Meursault's nose and trying to profit from the situation to possess the mind of the unfortunate accused: "Across the table he was already pushing the figure of Christ under my eyes and crying in an irrational way: 'I am a Christian. I ask pardon from Him for your faults. How can you not believe that He suffered for you?'" (*ET*, p. 1173). The scene is rather unlikely and even a caricature; there is a rancor discernible in it that goes beyond ordinary anticlericalism. What exasperates Camus is the magistrate's taking advantage of his official functions to impose his particular truth and, further, his drawing that truth ready-made from the ideology of his social class.

What must be done to save man is obviously to bar to the mind the way that gives birth to religions and to empires: "Man is that force that always ends up by wavering between gods and tyrants" (*LA*, p. 228). If religions have any use it is that they, precisely through reaction to them, give rise to that liberating force: "A revolution is always accomplished against the gods . . . The notion of a personal god-creator, and therefore responsible for all things, alone gives meaning to human protest. Thus one can say, and without paradox, that the history of revolt in the western world is inseparable from that of Christianity" (*HR*, p. 46). Was not Christianity itself in its origins animated by the spirit of revolt? Better still, it had favored the sudden appearance of individual consciousness by locating the source of salvation within the soul and promoting the notion of personal responsibility; it helped our lucidity to mature. But it subjugated destiny itself to religions, it became political, it codified itself, it became fixed, and henceforth the vital forces to which it owed its birth (according to Camus) acted in opposition to it.

These ideas are not original. They can be found from Proudhon* to Malraux; Dostoevski often lent such words to his characters. Still, they found an attentive listener in Camus, who gave them new life, as it were, through the vigor of his conviction and the prestige of his writing. The same may be said for another theme of indictment of which Feuerbach is considered the originator and that Camus found in Nietzsche.

Religion is in its essence a *passion for life*, it tends toward a *more-than-being:* "Myths are to religion what poetry is to truth; ridiculous masks placed over the passion for life" (*N*, p. 91). While visiting the Franciscan monastery so marvelously perched on the hillside of Fiesole, Camus discovered that positive aspect of the religious vocation: beyond all exclusively moral values, what the monk seeks is to exist with greater intensity. There is no sacrilege in comparing the rough homespun of the recluses of Fiesole to the attire of the young Florentines or to the flowers of the Tuscan prairies. It is always a matter, with sensuality and with asceticism, of bringing life to a certain "temperature." Up to this point the young Camus had no objection; on the contrary, he felt himself in Barrésian** or Gidian harmony with beings who entered the monastery only in order to live a life of intensity. But is it really that way, and is there not a misdeal? Would religion not tap these forces only to

* Pierre Joseph Proudhon (1809–1865), a political and economic theorist best known for his proposals for land-ownership reforms in *Qu'est-ce que la propriété* (1840) [trans. note].
** See note, p. 47.

alienate them immediately? And would it not be the greatest of deceits? Here we meet once again Feuerbach and his
successors: "If there is a sin against life it is not perhaps so
much to despair of it as it is to hope for another life and so
evade the implacable grandeur of this one . . ." (N, p. 69).
Thus Camus reproaches Christianity for devaluating the
Earth, for "veiling the beauty of the world and of faces"
and of postponing to an invisible future all that which
imparts value to present life. Man has invented another
world in order to vilify this one, in order to be able to rid
himself of an odious present and to direct his "intensity of
life" upon imperishable values.

God, like History, is only the "mirror" of man who, by
his own act, defrauds himself of what is best in him, his
happiness, by engulfing it in a vertical transcendance
(God) or in a horizontal one (the future). To resist religion, to stand opposed to the voracious myth of History, is
in both cases to help man come back into possession of
himself. We have already seen in Camus, and we will see it
again in him, an attachment to the present moment, an
enhancement of the ephemeral, that is diametrically contrary to religions as well as to philosophies of History. He
owed that to his positive and sensual temperament, he owed
it to Gide, to Montherlant, to Malraux. Vigny's verse,
"Love what one shall never see twice,"* assumed a fever-
ish resonance in this man haunted by the omnipresence of
death. It is this marvelous love of the fugitive moment that
is in his eyes the true proof of an ardent life. And, on the
contrary, the religious soul concerned with its paradise, the
militant prey to his dreams of absolute justice are the exiles
of life; it is they, in the last analysis—and Camus liked that
paradoxical inversion—who are the materialists: "The most

* La Maison du Berger, line 182.

repugnant materialism is not that which one thinks, but indeed that which attempts to pass off on us dead ideas for living realities and to divert to sterile myths the obstinate and lucid attention we give to that in us which must die forever" (*N*, p. 86). Inescapable death renders passing things valuable, confering upon them the infinite worth of what is destined to nothingness.

Religion in Greece did not have, Camus tells us, that effect of alienation which is endemic to religions of salvation. Man felt at home in a universe peopled by personal forces, both propitious and hostile, to whom one could pray, whom one could adore or curse. To History's profit, Christianity broke off men's consenting acceptance of their natural condition. For the ancients, the true life was that of the here and now, and the life of the dead was only a spectral survival. Jewish messianism, taken up by Christianity, emptied, so to speak, present life of its meaning. Those who live after the advent of Christianity and whom the Christian faith has deserted have no other resource than to turn to History and to transfer to it all the hope that centuries of faith had awakened in them. Otherwise there is only despair . . . "The greater part of men, except believers of every kind, are deprived of any future. They are reduced to the life of dogs up against a wall" (*Combat*, January, 1949.* It is this wall that Camus was to try to

---

* M. Onimus cites an article by Camus from "*Combat*, janvier 1949," which reads: "La plupart des hommes, sauf les croyants de toute espèce, sont privés d'avenir. Ils en sont réduits à la vie des chiens devant un mur." In fact, however, Camus published no articles in *Combat* in 1949. A remark very similar to the one cited by M. Onimus is contained in *Actuelles I* (Pléiade edition, p. 331); dated November, 1946, it reads: ". . . la plupart des hommes (sauf les croyants de toutes espèces) sont privés d'avenir. Il n'y a pas de vie valable sans

breach: we shall see how. Everything happens as if, in fact, religion had deprived men of their "honor" in delivering them over "completely to the humiliations of the divine" (*MS*, p. 182), in questioning their citizenship in this world, in inculcating in them a state of mind of "displaced persons" or of exiles in a vale of tears.

Owing to a vice inherent in his faith, the Christian seems incapable of participating wholly in the life and the struggle of other men: Father Paneloux exhausts himself in the "sanitary squads" and collaborates with those who combat the plague, but all in vain, for he remains like a stranger in their midst. His hope in another life makes of him, no matter what, an accomplice of Evil; his struggle cannot be as complete, as *despairing* as that of the unbeliever. For Camus, hope is always, in whatever guise it presents itself, a way of escaping from the present and, therefore, of living less. Here one recognizes a well known Nietzschean theme, a paradoxical eulogy of nihilism in that it exalts life. The death of hope calls upon us to create values—humble as they may be—and the destruction of every ideal puts an end to alienation; man emerges triumphant from that immense ruin. Strange optimism that excludes the future and

---

projection sur l'avenir, sans promesse de mûrissement et de progrès. Vivre contre un mur, c'est la vie des chiens. Eh bien! les hommes de ma génération et de celle qui entre aujourd'hui dans les ateliers et les facultés ont vécu et vivent de plus en plus comme des chiens." (". . . the majority of men [except for believers of all kinds] are deprived of a future. There is no worthwhile life without a projection into the future, without a promise of maturation and progress. To live with one's back to the wall is to live a dog's life. Well, then! the men of my generation, and of the one entering today into the factories and universities, have lived and still live more and more like dogs.") [trans. note].

thereby the sense of personal or collective life; the determination to tame the Absurd and to make of it his dwelling place, to sanctify the perishable and to embody in it the sacred. For Camus the "divine" exists; he felt it in the pure moments of ecstasy that we have already described. But this divine is *in* the world; it is to life what the flower is to the plant. In that ecstasy there is no desire to escape; the divinity that Camus encountered on the beaches of Algiers or on the terrace of his home at Loumarin is not associated with immortality and promises of salvation. It is composed of an intense *joie de vivre*. Camus asks us to look directly at the "truth of the body," that terrible and intoxicating truth where corruption and pleasure are fused into one, "for the body knows not hope" (*N*, p. 79). He gives us thus a lesson in obstinate courage: accept without evasions—with cold eyes and a serene heart. Such is "the impassiveness and the grandeur of the man without hope," the one extolled by another of Camus's masters, Vigny:

To moan, to weep, to pray is equally cowardly . . .*
It is the present whose value must be enhanced to equal that of the absolute by throwing oneself unstintingly into it with all one's love and all one's revolt: "a greater life and not another one" (*N*, p. 90). Religion offers too easy a refuge not to be suspect; and it is, paradoxically, this refuge of the timid that causes the most terrible of imperialisms to weigh upon men. Thus, through the weakness that it implies as through the violence that it exercises, religion is doubly destructive of that which is best and most vital in man.

It is even more destructive from a third point of view; and we confront here, along with the problem of Evil, the

---

* *La Mort du Loup*, line 85.

major objection over which Camus stumbled all his life. We have shown how on encountering old age, suffering, and death, he discovered the "other" side of things, that side which alone among living creatures men are, to their misfortune perhaps, capable of seeing. Even if he had not been, for other reasons, full of preconceived ideas with regard to religion, this scandal of Evil would probably have been enough to divorce him from it. Caught in the trap, he was never able to untangle this dilemma: either God does not exist and the world is absurd or God exists and it is He, then, who is evil. He would have willingly proclaimed with Proudhon: "God is evil," since we project in Him universal responsibility. Atheism is purely negative; it ascertains or affirms an absence. But antitheism attacks a hypothesis that it pretends to admit; it supposes for an instant the existence of God the better to affirm its rejection of Him: "I would rather remain with my unavenged suffering and my unsatisfied indignation," says Ivan Karamazov to Alyosha, *"even if I were wrong."** That is to say, the scandal of injustice would survive the indubitable revelation of God's existence, in which event it would be necessary to admit the horrible contradiction between justice and truth: "Perhaps it is better for God," murmurs Dr. Rieux, "that we not believe in Him and that we struggle with all our strength against death without raising our eyes to Heaven where He sits silent" (*LP*, p. 1321). Thus faith in God is instantly transformed into an indictment.

Camus thought of telling a story of a priest whose faith wavered in the presence of human suffering. This novelistic theme, which one finds in the *Carnets* (p. 213), reappears in the outlines for *La Peste:* Father Paneloux, in a prelimi-

---

* Fëdor Dostoevski, *The Brothers Karamazov*, trans. Constance Garnett (New York, 1950), p. 291.

nary version, was to have lost his faith. In fact, an early outline for *La Peste*, set down in April, 1941, read: "A young priest loses his faith in face of the black pus that flows from wounds. He takes his holy oils away. 'If I come through it alive . . .' But he will not make it" (*CN*, p. 230). In the final version, Paneloux does not lose his faith. On the contrary, he stiffens, clinging desperately to his belief, and his death is only the more troubling because of this. One wonders if, at the end of his strength, he did not want to die because he felt he was letting go. For he had been in the presence of something more terrible than pestiferous sores; it was not nausea that threatened to sweep away his confidence in God, but the death of a child. Like Ivan Karamazov, he comes face to face with indefensible injustice: the suffering of the innocent.

Father Paneloux's first reaction in the presence of the plague was to accuse men. His is the classic response, the easiest one, that of Job's friends: if God strikes you, it is because you are guilty. And in his sermon Paneloux invites the Oranais to make their "self-examinations." One can always admit one's guilt. There are nowhere, there will never be, any innocents, and so God is justified to everyone's satisfaction. Paneloux brings into play another well known argument: suffering is in the end good, for it purifies the soul and draws it nearer to God. "This very scourge that sears your flesh raises you up and shows you the way" (*LP*, p. 1927), and in pietistic terms he goes on to speak of that "exquisite brightness of eternity which lies at the depths of all suffering." At the outset of the epidemic he was able to pronounce such statements without causing a scandal. But as the plague spreads its ravages what spiritual meaning is to be found in those senseless heaps of corpses? Paneloux ventures a second sermon, this time adopting the tone and gestures of Job. When Job, who knows himself to be innocent, dares question God, when Father Paneloux finds himself affronted by an evil that indiscriminately carries off the good and the bad and kills little children, what response can one still possibly give? Father Paneloux, like Job and doubtless after Job's example, now preaches self-renunciation; it is the true, the only possible religious response. But from the "worldly" point of view it is no answer. Job simply renounced the will to understand. Where no logical, human response is possible there must be an *excess* of faith and confidence for one to bow one's head and love what God permits to happen. This is the virtue of acceptance; not any banal resignation but humiliation consented to out of love. If one follows the text of this second sermon closely, one can only pay homage to Camus's lucidity. Without participating in it himself, and on the contrary full of hesitations and revolt, he explains perfectly what is religion's virtue. A theologian could only approve the terms Paneloux uses right down to the nuances he is anxious to emphasize: neither resignation nor fatalism but crucifying acceptance joined with a will to struggle against Evil. Paneloux rejects easy explanations (the dead child will be eternally happy etc.). He admits there is "nothing more important on earth than a child's suffering and the horror attendant on it and the reasons that had to be found for it" (*LP*, p. 1400). But at the same time, through a gratuitous gesture, he renounces the asking of these reasons of God. It is *all or nothing;* one does not make a currency of one's faith, and if one believes in God one must remain silent and act.

Let us stop for a moment at this central point in Camus's reflections on religion.

From the "worldly" point of view (Camus's own), as

seen from the outside, Paneloux's attitude is simply inadmissible. It consists of "embracing that which devours," and it is a property of religious "alienation." Hope "in spite of everything" makes injustice an object of worship. To his German friend Camus declared: "You have chosen injustice, you have placed yourself on the side of the gods" (*LA*, p. 241). To take the side of the gods is to accept Destiny and since this Destiny is manifestly bad, to accept it is to accept Evil. But Christianity demands more; it demands love. Paneloux murmurs, " '. . . perhaps we must love what we cannot understand.' 'No, Father,' Rieux replies. 'I have another idea of love. And I shall refuse until death to love this creation where children are tortured' " (*LP*, p. 1395). In a strange tale whose explanation remains obscure, *Le Renégat* (*The Renegade*), Camus shows us a missionary of weak character being tortured by savages who are worshippers of evil. Terrified, brutalized, enslaved, the unfortunate man comes at last to worship the hideous idol, to become its devoted attendant, and to assassinate a new missionary who has come to convert the idolators (*ER*, pp. 1575–93). The tale is a terrible caricature of "those who love that which crushes them" (*MS*, p. 180) and persecute whoever seeks to free them from their humiliating bondage. Man alone is aware of injustice since he alone judges his own destiny; if he renounces revolt which is his honor and, so to speak, his mission, he ceases to be a man.

Now Christianity has made an injustice the keystone of its Redemption: is it not the spectacle of injustice that one adores on altars? An innocent—and what an innocent!—nailed on a cross. Is this not to proclaim the all-powerfulness of Evil? The Son of God had to take it upon Himself up to the point of death and almost to the point of despair.

Camus pondered this cardinal mystery of Christianity and
was by turns moved by it and indignant at it. He always
spoke of Christ Himself in terms of respect; is He not the
symbol of human misfortune? Jesus is merely another innocent that the representative of the God of Abraham exe-
cuted in a spectacular manner (*HR*, p. 53). Somewhat like
Socrates, a victim of religious sectarianism, Jesus, under
that human aspect, belongs to the world of martyred innocents and his fate should increase our revolt. He went clear
to the end of his misfortune and even, just before dying—
what is more frightful perhaps than death—he knew the
loss, it seems, of hope: "My God, why have you abandoned
me?" (*MS*, p. 146). Thus, seen by Camus, Christ incarnates
not God but "the perfect man" (*MS*, p. 146) precisely
because he attained the most absurd condition by dying for
an illusion. His life and death illustrate in exemplary fash-
ion the human condition, whose entire nobility consists in
giving itself to an ideal that has no value except through the
sacrifice that one consents to make for it. There is the
undying truth of Christianity that confirms for us our daily
experience: "If Christianity has touched us so deeply it is
through its God made man. But its truth and its greatness
end at the cross and at the moment when He cries his
surrender. Tear out the final page of the Gospel and you
have a human religion, a cult of solitude and of greatness is
offered to us. Of course, His bitterness makes Him unbearable. But therein is His truth and the falsehood of all the
rest" (*CN*, p. 206). If the final pages of the gospel are
ripped out (that is to say, the Resurrection and all the
miraculous elements that surround it) the story of Jesus has
"humanist" echoes such as one hears in the course of Greek
tragedies—an exaltation of injustice and suffering that penetrates so deeply that it purifies the soul and bestows upon

it the "majestic sadness" that comes in the aftermath of great misfortune. If Christianity stopped there it would confirm Sysiphus' bitterness. What is amazing in the Christian faith is that it has identified God with suffering and that it has made even of the Son of God's despair an object of mysterious adoration. If many religions have minimized suffering or have attempted to justify it by means of the "wheel" of existences, Christianity alone has placed it at the very center of its mysteries. "The night of Golgotha has so much importance in human history only because in those shadows divinity, ostensibly abandoning its traditional privileges, lived to the end, despair included, the anguish of death. Thus is explained the *Lama Sabacthani* and the terrifying doubt of Christ in agony. Agony would be a small thing if it were sustained by eternal hope. For God to be man He had to despair" (*HR*, p. 50). Camus returned several times to this supreme cry of Jesus. Even the sarcastic Clamence confesses himself touched: "he was not superhuman, you may believe me . . . He cried out his agony and that is why I admire him . . . who died without knowing" (*LC*, p. 1532). What did he find on the other side? For Camus the truth of the Gospel ended at that ninth hour when Jesus with a great outcry yielded up His soul. All the rest is only a "betrayal" or an imposture through which religion metamorphoses evil into an object of love. No, it was not lessons of charity that Camus drew from the death of Jesus, but rather an intensification of his revolt: "Jesus frustrated is just one more innocent . . . The abyss that separates the master from the slaves opens forthwith."*

And we are returned, beyond the drama of Calvary, to

* M. Onimus does not give any source for this citation [trans. note].

the mystery of God. Christianity, "in order to answer in advance all the Cains of the world," has attempted "to soften the face of God." The soft shadings of Christianity rubbed away, God resumes his horrid visage, that of a mad tyrant. The term is not excessive. For it is impossible to escape the dilemma: either men are free and guilty but God not all-powerful, or men are not free and then the responsibility of God is commensurate with Universal Evil (*MS*, p. 79). The hypothesis of an all-powerful God implied for Camus that of a cruel or merely indifferent God for whom the suffering and death of children and the innocent are without importance.

Like Victor Hugo in the depths of his mourning, Camus envisions a distant, inhuman God, stranger to all that moves and interests us. In *Le Malentendu* he incarnated Him in that supposedly mute old servant who watches the frightful drama take shape without doing anything to stop it. He speaks out only once, at the moment the curtain falls, when everything is lost: Maria has thrown herself on her knees, she has uttered that cry which is a supplication: "Oh my God, I cannot live in this wilderness . . . Have pity on me . . . Grant me your aid . . ." (*LM*, pp. 179–80). Then the old man deigns to open his mouth, but only in order to say: "No!" The effect is perhaps facile; it illustrates in any case that "eternal silence" which is for Camus the sinister attribute of divinity. Man is abandoned in a universe where his voice remains without echo. There is no one anywhere—or if there is Someone, it can only be, judging by appearances, a maleficent and heartless spirit. "Pray to your god," Martha cries, "that He make you like stone. He takes happiness for Himself," and it is once more by a stone that Camus symbolizes the divine in that terrible tale, *La Pierre qui pousse*, where we see a man spend his strength carrying a heavy stone as a consequence of a superstitious vow. The stone weighs down upon the man as God, with all His absurd or lunatic mass, hangs above us: "Oh! I hate this world where we are reduced to God . . ." (LM, p. 171). What does such blasphemy mean? That we shall be slaves on our earth for as long as we see fit to recognize in it a creation. The Face that appears as soon as one imagines a Consciousness behind what we call Destiny is not a face of goodness; it is the grimacing face of one of those idols on which certain peoples have instinctively inscribed the stigmata of hatred, stupidity, and cruelty. "If Caligula is carried away with bloody madness," Jean Grenier dares write, "it is in imitation of nature, which indiscriminately slaughters everyone."* Thus "the imitation of God" renders one irrational. On the contrary, it is in his struggle against such a God that man can found order and justice; antitheism becomes an elementary need of the conscience. For Camus, therefore, the Christian who claims to love God could never be perfectly sincere. How can Christianity's famous charity accept without hesitation the scandal of Evil? Is it possible to be Christian in all frankness without —unconsciously at least—making evasions? Must one not be blind or deprived of all feeling to dare love Him who has allowed to swarm over the earth "the bacillus of the plague that does not die nor ever disappear" (LP, p. 1472)?

It remains to explain for what reasons Camus developed a view of Christianity calculated to disconcert Christians and one that rendered their faith totally unacceptable to himself.

Let us note first of all that Camus's first intellectual

---

* "Préface" to Théâtre, Récits, Nouvelles, p. xii.

contact with the phenomenon of religion took place in his philosophy courses and under the influence of Jean Grenier. To judge by certain passages in *Les Iles*, Grenier was much attracted to the "disincarnate" religions of India, where the opposition between earthly life and God is complete and permanent. "One must choose between the world and God. The world may be reached only through the world and God through God."* Camus met such perspectives in Saint Augustine, Pascal, and Kierkegaard; it is impossible to go to God *by way of* the world, through attempting to spiritualize the temporal. One must then shrug off the world as one takes off clothing, making oneself "indifferent to man" so as to appear stripped but pure before the Absolute.

Christianity could have brought to Camus an entirely different revelation—that of an incarnate religion in the example of Christ, who could have appeared to him as a model of restraint opposed to a certain religious excess, since He shares equally in himself the human and the divine, remaining fully God while at the same time assuming and thereby consecrating the human condition in His integrality. Camus did not encounter this Christian humanism. The Christianity that he knew was that of the "hidden God," a tragic religion for which God is not a proximate, adorable presence, the Father of the prodigal son, but a distant God—very far away and entirely incomprehensible —who is attainable only through torture or a twist of reasoning, through a pure act of faith. Such a religion is founded on the creature's feeling of abjection, of his irremediable fall, and of the unfathomable omnipotence of a God whom we cannot judge according to the standards of

* *Les Iles*, p. 135.

our justice. It is natural that so mutilating a faith should give rise, as its consequence, to a "humanistic" revolt, all the more atheistic in that God has been placed further away in a still stranger world.

We have already noted that Camus was poorly acquainted with living Christianity as it is practiced daily. At the age of twenty-two, in 1936, at Professor René Poirier's instigation, he wrote a thesis for the Diplôme d'Etudes Supérieures on Plotinus and Augustine: *Métaphysique chrétienne et néoplatonisme*. This young man who knew so little of Christian life was thus plunged without preparation into Augustinian thought, discovering all that it can contain of somberness and discouragement in the eyes of a nonbeliever excluded a priori from "grace." This first contact left an indelible trace. A friend of his later years has confided that Camus continued to be "very shocked by the theory of Saint Augustine on hell and on the fate of unbaptized children after death."* We will cite only one passage from this thesis, but a significant one: "If it is true that man is nothing and that his destiny is entirely in God's hands, that works do not suffice to assure man of his reward, if the 'Nemo bonus'** is valid, who then shall attain this kingdom of God? The distance is so great from man to God that no one can hope to cross it. Man cannot succeed in it and despair alone is open to him. But then the Incarnation brings its solution. Man being unable to reach God, God comes down to him."*** In this text, which is to the letter

* M. Onimus does not name the source of this remark [trans. note].

** *Nemo bonus:* "No one is good . . . ," a reference to Mark 10:18, "Why dost thou call me good? No one is good but God only" [trans. note].

*** *Métaphysique chrétienne et néoplatonisme*, p. 1237.

of perfect orthodoxy, resound two words of importance for us: the *distance* between man and God and the necessity of coming near to *despair*. If one ever places exaggerated emphasis on what separates us from Him, God retreats from us and the Absurd looms up, growing even larger. Then the ineluctable option, Paneloux's "all or nothing," imposes itself: either one takes up one's abode in the Absurd and faces up vigorously to the monster, or one must believe in the "miracle" which amounts to total submission and silence. It is thus that Camus understood Pascal and was disposed to understand Kierkegaard. Such were his masters of Christian doctrine; paradoxically, it was under the inspiration of the most austere Christianity that his antitheism and combative humanism were nourished.

In an article on Jean Guitton's *Le Portrait de M. Pouget*, Camus wrote, in 1943: *"We must choose between miracles and the Absurd.* There is no middle ground. The choice Pascal made is well enough known."* Camus's choice is no less known. But in both cases there was a choice, a free decision, which forces the believer to pronounce Tertullian's inhuman words: *Credo quia absurdum.*** One cannot overstate the total absence of love in these relations between Camus and the divine; everything devolves on the intellectual level, in a rarified atmosphere of coldness and lucidity. The God he glimpsed was a philosopher's god—an idea, not a presence. It is not impossible that he knew Saint Augustine before he knew the Gospels. In the Gos-

---

* *Portrait d'un élu, Cahiers du sud*, no. 225 (April, 1943), p. 306.

** *Credo quia absurdum*, "I believe it because it is absurd," a remark from the *De carne christi* of Tertullian (155?–?220), an early Christian apologist. This phrase was long attributed incorrectly to Augustine [trans. note].

pels he was never *to feel* the human echo of the parables
and divine tenderness; his expectations were answered on
the contrary by the cry of Jesus and the night of choice:
the absurd death of the Man crucified or the mystery-
shrouded Resurrection. A correspondence was formed in
his mind between the irrational and the pious, between
lunacy and faith.

From that point on one cannot exaggerate the importance of Kierkegaard, read with passion but not without
some preconceptions, beginning in 1936. Camus discovered
in the Danish thinker the dazzling confirmation of what he
had found in Saint Augustine and Pascal: an intransigent
Christianity supported by a faith which alone remains
standing in the universal debris without the support of
reason, without the warmth of the fire of love. It must be
remembered that Kierkegaard sought to defend the faith
against Hegel's humanism as Pascal wanted to protect it
against the humanism of the *libertins*.* Both thus thought
to serve it through their pessimism; they have often succeeded in weakening it by suspending it in emptiness. Father de Lubac has shown very well the symptoms of de-
generation hidden in that, one might say, too fanatically
religious consciousness: "Rather than nourishment, Kierkegaard's thought is a tonic, and taken in too large doses it
could become toxic. He who, thinking to follow him,
should happen to enclose himself straight off within Kierkegaard's positions would risk shutting himself off from all
rational life, perhaps from every culture, an inhuman attitude which was not Kierkegaard's and from which Christi-

---

* The *libertin* movement represented a strong current of
seventeenth-century French free-thinkers who were either
atheistic or who seriously questioned the validity of orthodox
Christian doctrine [trans. note].

anity would in the final analysis draw no advantage." An understatement: far from drawing advantage from it, Christianity is denatured by contact with desperate irrationalism. It is risky business to claim to derive eternal hope from despair; it is a "romantic" and a precarious attitude. Religion, in this case, is based only on a paradoxical "leap" at the last second, a leap that rejects the Absurd for belief in God. "For Chestov (author of a book on *Kierkegaard et la philosophie existentielle*, published in 1936) reason is vain but there is something beyond reason. For an absurd intellect reason is vain and there is nothing beyond reason" (*MS*, p. 55). Thus extreme faith-on-trust leads to extreme nihilism. Camus's example shows clearly how imprudent it would be to found an apologetic on the negations of existentialism, for to admit that faith demands philosophical suicide razes its foundations. As Camus very accurately saw it: "This God is sustained only by the negations of human reason." This brings us back to Father Paneloux's terms: "Leap to the heart of the unacceptable . . . *choose* to hate God or to love him . . ." (*LP*, p. 1403). After the example of Kierkegaard's Abraham summoned by God to slay his only son in order to proclaim his faith, Paneloux dares to declare from the heights of his pulpit that we must wish for the suffering of a child since God wishes it (*LP*, p. 1403). Is it not at the extreme limits of horror that faith is best able to burst forth?

In his *Carnets*, Camus compares that ultimate and almost desperate faith to a screen: "In the Italian museums the little painted screens the priest held before the faces of condemned men so that they might not see the scaffold. The existential leap is the screen" (*CN*, p. 178). There is on the one side the decidedly irrational reality and, on the other, a will to delude oneself, a forced hope, a religious embezzlement which is nothing at bottom but trickery. To substitute for his cry of revolt a "frenzied adhesion" (*MS*, p. 58), is to succeed in no longer seeing the Absurd in order to provide oneself some manner of comfort. "I do not want to build anything on the incomprehensible" (*MS*, p. 60), declares Camus. Such structures are nothing but mirages and the Kierkegaardian "rehearsal"—to one who views it from outside it is only a "pathetic juggler's act" (*MS*, p. 54).

More serious still: the image of God when it emerges from the Absurd remains marked by it with indelible traces. Camus observed this very well. Kierkegaard went to God not according to the categories of goodness and beauty; he reaches Him "behind the empty and hideous faces of His indifference, of His injustice and His hatred . . ." (*MS*, p. 183). "Through a tortured subterfuge he gives to the irrational the face, and to his God the attributes of the Absurd: unjust, capricious and incomprehensible" (*MS*, p. 58). Decidedly, "the absurd, which is the metaphysical state of the conscious man, does not lead to God" (*MS*, p. 60). We will subscribe willingly to that statement, but the basic hypothesis is disputable. For having parted from the Kierkegaardian hypothesis Camus had paradoxically closed off access to a Christian knowledge of God.

Did Dostoevski provide Camus with a more evangelical image of Christianity? Not at all. The sentimental and almost sensual mysticism in the works of the Russian novelist served to confirm Camus in his prejudices. Nothing solid, vertebrate in the faith of a Zossima, an Alexis, or a Myshkin. And there is scarcely any difference between the ecstasies of an atheist like Kirillov and those of Alyosha; for all its being no longer tragic but passionate instead, irrationalism is none the less suspect. The intellect, wrote Gide, is for Dostoevski "the enemy of the kingdom of God, life eternal, and that bliss where time is not, reached only by renouncing the individual self and sinking deep in a solidarity that knows no distinction."* There would thus be in him "an evangelical depreciation of the intellect" that is on the same level as the irrationalism of his Danish contemporary. If Myshkin is the model of a truly religious soul, must we consecrate sickness, maladroitness, and failure? Moreover, for Camus, Dostoevski was personally very much nearer to his rebels than to his chosen ones. The interpretation that he gives that ambiguous body of work is both partial and significant. He draws the novelist to himself and lends to him personally the words of a Stavrogin or an Ivan. But it is perhaps to Kirillov that Camus owes the most, that mystic without God who tries to open up to man an infinity on Earth by delivering him from fear, by carrying, through the sacrifice he makes of his life, the weight of all human anguish, a kind of latter-day Christ, the founder of a kingdom where men would at last be at home. In fact, Dostoevski, torn between life in God and life outside Him, furnished Camus the example of that *all or nothing*, dividing his fictional creation into two worlds of which one does not always know which is really his. Dostoevski went all the way in both directions, to absolute faith and to antitheism, choosing finally, it seems, an irrational faith. It was not Christianity but rather the Nietzsche "before the fact" that Camus appreciated in Dostoevski; it was his rebels and his "demons" that inspired him.

It is essential for our discussion to indicate the significance for Camus of his encounter in 1946 with the work of

* André Gide, *Dostoyevsky* (New York: New Directions, 1961), p. 127.

Simone Weil.* Unfortunately, documents concerning this point are disappointingly few. That Camus was interested in Weil is certain: it was on his advice that Gallimard published her *L'Enracinement* in 1949. Both were lucid and exigent minds, both had suffered from the "misfortune of the world" and felt bound up in that misfortune; both were born with a passion for justice that is in reality a passion for charity; both were anguished beings fascinated by the awareness of Evil and less sensitive to hope than to a form of despair that is highly personal but common to the two of them; both had the same love of Greece and Greek thought, of Plato and of a certain Socratism. It is very probable, if not certain, that the perpetual allusions to "Greek wisdom" scattered throughout Camus's works after 1948 owe much to Simone Weil. She confirmed him in the idea that Europe would not escape from History and its inevitability except through a return to "that superior equilibrium that brought the harmony of numbers even into the tragedy of bloodshed."** With the same hatred both Camus and Simone Weil attacked all forms of imperialism, orthodoxy, established churches, and all that appeared to enslave the spirit or to facilitate its resignation; each was endowed with a conscience tempted by revolt but seeking to go beyond the negations that revolt implies.

But at that point they part ways. Camus believed in happiness. He celebrated it in lyrical and sometimes almost despairing terms; Simone Weil did not believe in it and placed all her expectations in grace alone, in a salvation come from Elsewhere. At the extreme limits of lucidity, the

* See *Essais* (Pléiade edition), pp. 1699 ff.
** M. Onimus does not give any source for this citation [trans. note].

soul swings suspended in faith or in ardent fervor, in detachment or in the "fury of living" and always, at the bottom, there is Kierkegaard or Nietzsche. Weil and Camus meet like two opposing versants that join at their summit only to diverge immediately. The same vision of an atrocious world produced in one a stoic and humanistic reaction: he constructed the kingdom of man. The other shut herself up in that suffering and there she met the crucified Lord. One attempted desperately to build on emptiness, the other made of the very emptiness a fullness.

The Christian truth—like every living truth—is at the intersection of two vectors that diverge although they originate from the same fundamental mystery of the Incarnation. According to the times, temperaments, education, even race, certain Christians have been led to emphasize in the Incarnation the humiliation of the physical being, a model of suffering assumed. They go to Christ by the Way of the Cross. Others are more sensitive to that in the Incarnation which is, on the contrary, glorious for a nature that the insertion of the divine into the temporal came to consecrate and exalt. They do not envision the Christ of Calvary as foremost but rather the Christ of the Nativity and the Resurrection.

Because of his background and his personal affinities, Camus accustomed himself to the first image. He found in it an echo, it seemed, of his own painful and poverty-stricken experience. But he found in it at the same time—and for him it was an insurmountable obstacle—a devaluation and even a radical condemnation of human values and human effort. Such a religion became the enemy of man since it founded salvation on the empty insignificance of the temporal, since it consented to bestow the gift of hope only after having reduced the individual to despair. When,

in the face of a child's death, Rieux declares that he will
always reject a creation where children are tortured, Father
Paneloux, "a stricken shadow" on his face, murmurs: "Ah,
Doctor, I have just come to understand what we call
grace!" (*LP*, p. 1395). What is there to say? It is that the
grace bestowed on Paneloux allows him to accept injustice
—not without personal upheaval, of course—but finally to
accept it. Now, justice is the order that men impose on
chaos; is not the little justice that reigns on Earth their
pride and their justification? Christianity has certainly
served man in awakening his conscience to the existence of
Evil, in thus infusing into his soul the seeds of revolt, but
from this point one must go on beyond a form of acceptance that leads only to alienation. Camus's objections are
not, unlike those of the Christian "modernists," of an historical order; it matters little to him that the Gospels may
have been interpolated or that they contradict one another.
His quarrel takes place, above and beyond any exegesis, on
the level of principles. Modern agnosticism is founded
rather on "a passionate refusal to believe" than on rational-
istic arguments of a philosophical or historical order. It is a
question of defending man against an enterprise that tends
to divert him from his earthly task and that threatens to
weaken the vigor of his revolt.

There is in all this a misunderstanding for which Christian teaching, entirely suffused in the West with Augustinian and Jansenist concepts, is in great part responsible.
From Pascal to Simone Weil, Camus met only with a paradoxical faith, founded on a destructive lucidity that, like his
own, was bent on creating a void. Now, Christianity runs
entirely contrary to any negation of the world and man;
but Camus never came to know this "versant" of joy and

hope, illuminated by the love of God. He did not open either a Claudel or a Péguy nor, with all the more reason, a Teilhard de Chardin. To Camus, the Christian God seemed to be a stranger totally removed from the world, Christianity a rending asunder of the soul, never a fullness.

3

An Atheistic Humanism

The Temptation of Nihilism

Camus's constant effort, after he had taken cognizance of the consequences of the rejection of God, was to surmount the absurdism and nihilism that that rejection implies. This effort he termed "revolt," and with him this word took on a positive meaning; for him it always implies a going beyond a simple *no*.

Two periods, separated by the war of 1940: in the second, the "going beyond" led to a generous humanism provoked and inspired by the fact of the war itself. In the first period, however, the outcome of the struggle had remained doubtful. Externally, Camus seems to have been seized by a sharp appetite for activity. He pursued his studies at the Faculty of Letters while at the same time directing a theatrical group, *L'Equipe*, which he had founded, and earning his living through a dozen different jobs—weatherman, prefectural employee, seller of automobile accessories. He plunged into politics (he joined the Communist Party in 1934), and then he collaborated on a leftist newspaper, *Alger-Républicain*, that he had helped to found and through which he engaged in resounding campaigns in behalf of the Algerian "natives" and against the abuses of the colonial regime. In short, an active man, full of promise, happy. His friends at *L'Equipe* recall a man full of life, his collaborators on *Alger-Républicain*, a serious young man possessed by an ideal of justice and proud to fight for that ideal.

However, when one looks at the *Carnets* and the works of that period, another Camus is revealed—a mind that makes an effort to think against itself, against its vital instinct and its idealistic hopes. "What appears to me so evident, I must support even against myself" (*MS*, p. 74). Caught in the trap of sincerity, his idealism, out of a scrupulous sense of honesty, worked to undermine his own values. Camus was to make every effort to live and to survive in a state of "continuous revolution," that is to say in a perpetual state of questioning.

Thus, in his severity toward himself, Camus could not shut himself up like a simple militant in the ideal for which he fought. An imperious voice forced him to unlearn hope and backed him up against the wall of scepticism: "It is profoundly immaterial whether one fights windmills or giants" (*CN*, p. 185), wrote this singular enthusiast, comparing himself ironically to Don Quixote, and this apostle confesses that "in this great temple deserted by the gods all [his] idols have feet of clay" (*N*, p. 101). This impassioned disciple of justice took arms against all values: "Our time is dying from having believed in values and that things could be beautiful and cease being absurd" (*CN*, p. 43). Nothing, to take him fully at his word, has any meaning really and, consequently, in face of the human desire for rationality, everything is profoundly tragic and nothing is truly serious . . .

These successive and sometimes simultaneous attitudes of Camus toward the Absurd are interrelated like the acts of a tragedy. It is this tragedy of atheism that we now undertake to depict.

Despair immobilizes: her sorrow turned Niobe into stone. On the other hand, a consciousness that cultivates its own lucidity thinks it sees in the compact solidity of stone the image of repose. An object does not think or hope or despair: it contains within it a fullness that is its perfection; it is what it is, totally and completely. The animal also (and one recalls here the cat Mouloud, celebrated by Grenier).* To live fully is perhaps to forget that one is living at all, to have no longer the desire to think or to be moved, to live on sensations alone. To hope, to expect something and even to desire it, whatever it may be, would this not be finally to sin against life? "Extraordinary instant when spirituality repudiates morality, when happiness is born of the absence of hope, when the mind finds its reason in the body" (*N*, p. 97). From moments of this kind Meursault was born, the man whose life does not respond to the great questions but renders them useless because he lives, under the sun, a mediocre life that satisfies him but remains far from the hopes and great vocations that lift up humanity.

Camus's position with respect to Meursault is ambiguous and, what is more, changed. In writing *L'Etranger* (1940–1942), one would say he rid himself of a temptation. For what is Meursault finally? An *alienated* person, enough of a *stranger* to himself and to other men to be able to denounce, by means of that very distance, the scurrilous

* See note, p. 49.

horror of the "inauthentic" life. Meursault's life is not acceptable, and that of the superficial people who surround him is even less so: such a book is the angry work of a man who became aware of an absence that nothing can console. Meursault's indifference denounces, at one and the same time the poverty of conventional sentimentalism (with which men try to ornament—and to hide—their existence) and the horror of a lucid mind for whom things would be only what they truly are. Meursault's positivism and the facile idealism of "pure souls" are similarly intolerable. Of all Camus's stories, *L'Etranger* is probably the most oppressive because it offers no way out. His hero is a totally impoverished being; in seeing him live one is convinced that all is nothing but façade and that behind the scenes there also is nothing. Meursault provokes us by his lack of humanity, but, in return, that very lack of humanity unmasks our illusions. Camus was to say that he "dies for the truth" (*PL/I*, p. 1920), but what truth? A negative truth, to wit, that the world, that life, has no sense and that there is no truth except the sun and the noontime *apéritif*. Meursault lives (or rather wants to live) without "shadows," that is to say, without mystery and dreams, in the immediate, and this breaks up at once into the sordid and the insignificant. His friend Céleste proclaims ingenuously: "He's a man"; but if Meursault is a man then human life is impossible. His "innocence" is equal to that of the living robots he observes from his balcony on Sunday afternoons; the innocence of an insect or a bird, and society, like the old peoples' home, is only a "dull chattering of parakeets." The horror of life oozes from all the pores of this apparently cold tale, a hatred of man, a scorn for that which fills his pitiable life: the projects, the hopes, the loves . . . . The world seen by

Meursault resembles those deathstruck cities painted by Bernard Buffet, with their blank houses and deserted streets.

However, this man is adjusted to his absurd existence; he has need of nothing else, and one must imagine him happy, in much the way that Sisyphus was. Now, it is precisely that absence of anything else that is insupportable. Such a life is not *Life*. The entire story suggests this, and thus it merges with the tragic. In this character Camus embodied both his Kingdom (the simple joys, women, the cinema, bathing in the sea, the sun, the frugal and laborious life) and his Exile (the atrocity of an unfathomable existence, dry, stultifying, stupid). In his resentment, he comes close to Meursault, as Clamence later was to feel himself attracted to the thug: "When one has by profession and by inclination meditated much upon man it happens that he experiences a nostalgic affection for the primates: they, they at least, do not have mental reservations" (*LC*, p. 1476). "The stupid felicity of stones" (*LM*, p. 179)* is the ultimate expression of nihilism, and it is certainly nihilism that such an existence proclaims: "The guy who showed every promise and who now works in a office. He does nothing anywhere else, going home, going to bed, waiting for the dinner hour while smoking, going to bed again . . . Thus all year long. He waits. He waits to die. Of what use is the promise since in any case . . ." (*PL*, p. 1906). Would the man without a conscience be the only happy man because nothing touches him, nothing disturbs

* M. Onimus cites this phrase from the earlier version of *Le Malentendu:* "la stupide félicité de cailloux"; in the final version (Pléiade edition, pp. 109–180), Camus changed this to "le bonheur stupide des cailloux" ("the stupid happiness of stones") [trans. note].

him, because he is not visited by *anxiety?* Camus was several times tempted to commit this sin against the mind. His mother exemplified for him a stoicism of silence that he found again elsewhere in the Islamic *mektoub.* The man who wrote *Noces* and *Le Mythe de Sisyphe,* one after the other, speaks of a "profound indifference which is," he said, "in me like a natural infirmity." An ascetic and haughty indifference that turns to the "sanctity of negation," to "heroism without God," and that defines a certain life where courage mingles with lassitude. Whatever the origin, be it instinctive or voluntary, indifference is a numbing of the consciousness, that consciousness "by which everything begins and which gives everything its value" (*MS*, p. 27). It destroys, then, what is most precious to man—his appetite for transcendence—and makes a thing of him. Sheltered under that cloak, the human being no longer hears any call. He installs himself severely and bitterly in his successively changing reality, he clings to it. Let no one try to dislodge him from it! Meursault detests having questions posed to him, and when his homicidal act yanks him out of his shell he redoubles his indifference and scorn, he becomes a spectator of his own drama in order not to participate in it. Up to the very last moment, Meursault will refuse to enter into the others' game, he will remain glued to objects, to the evening calm, to the peace of summer nights; he will continue to live as a stranger, as a sleep-walker, as he has always done, and his misfortune will not render him tragic but simply hunted—like an animal at bay —on the margin of humanity and full of scorn for it.

This book can only be the work of a sorrowful soul and of a divided will. Between 1936 and 1940 Camus passed through crises of which the novel *La Mort heureuse* (*The Happy Death*—which the *Carnets* reveal he had begun thinking about in 1936) bears the trace. *L'Etranger* resulted from it since it develops one of the aspects of *La Mort heureuse*, the first one entitled "Natural Death." Mersault, the protagonist of *La Mort heureuse*, like his successor Meursault, led a routine, banal, inauthentic life. In order to bring him back to himself, his mentor Zagreus furnishes him with the opportunity to commit a crime: Zagreus (this name of a god who died and returned to life is obviously symbolic) has himself killed by his own disciple! In what follows, boredom, travel, sickness separate Mersault more and more from his original innocence and condemn him finally to suicide. The incoherence of this long story shows that *L'Etranger* is situated at the center of eddies that threw its author in turn toward anguish or toward the position of indifference. But in both cases he met only death and never, whatever he may say, "happy death."

Caligula (in the play of the same name begun in 1938 and staged in 1945) is exactly the contrary of Meursault. If one is nothing but indifference, the other is pure consciousness. He thinks, and he sees what Meursault refuses to see and to think upon, and that knowledge drives him mad. But his madness is less outrageous than indifference—more human since it results from lucidity. Caligula touched the corpse of his beloved Drusilla; then he withdrew, trembling, and disappeared. When he returns to the imperial palace he is no longer the same man: he has come to know Evil. The words that he pronounces then are very simple but heavy with significance: "I suddenly felt a need for the impossible, things as they are do not seem to me satisfactory . . . this world the way it is made is not bearable" (*CL*, p. 15). He gives himself the task of awakening men to what he has seen, of teaching them the truth about life. He will answer evil with evil, disorder with an excess of disorder and, since he is emperor and all-powerful, he will place irrationality on the throne because it, as well, is mistress of the world. "The longing for truth at any price is a passion that spares nothing and which nothing can resist" (*LC*, p. 1515), a destructive passion that leads to suicide since the ultimate truth is that there is no truth and realizing this engenders hatred of life, cruelty, sadism. Caligula amasses crimes since "there is only one way to equal the gods: one has only to be as cruel as they . . . I have assumed the foolish and incomprehensible face of the gods" (*CL*, pp. 67 and 69). This he does without joy, simply in order to be coherent with the incoherence of things. This buffoon, who pretends to play with all that is most serious, is a man in despair whose laugh is never anything but a paroxysm of anguish. "Love, Caesonia, I have learned that it was noth- ing . . . To live, Caesonia, to live is the contrary of loving . . ." (*CL*, p. 28). Terrifying words through which ap- pear, it seems, Camus's own great disappointment and his thirst for something else. "O Caesonia, I knew that one could despair but I did not know what that word meant. I believed like everyone that it was a sickness of the soul. But no, it is the body that suffers. My skin hurts, my chest, my limbs. My head bursts and my heart swells with disgust . . . How hard, how bitter it is to become a man" (*CL*, p. 26). For man carries within him a need that nothing in the world can satisfy: "If I had had the moon, if love sufficed, everything would be changed" (*CL*, p. 107). Caligula is a mystic for whom pitiful human happiness cannot suffice since it has limits and we still must die. When Caesonia says to him: "It can be so good to live and to love in the purity of one's heart," he responds, not without pride: "Each finds his purity where he can. For me, it lies in pursuing the essential" (*CL*, p. 102). Certainly Caligula is not modest—

modesty, he says, "is the only sentiment that I shall perhaps never experience" (CL, p. 66). But must we reproach him for it? Scipion lacks such pride and that is why he can still marvel and communicate with the beauty of the world: the cries of the swallows in the evening air are enough to make him happy. Caligula has other needs.

Happily, in contrast to Caligula there is Cherea, the mature man who, no less lucid than the adolescent emperor (and therefore less despairing), has learned from experience what man's suffering is, and he refuses to add to it. Cherea knows that there are "limits" beyond which all dignity disappears. Caligula possesses the radicalism of youth; for him it is all or nothing; since everything is impossible, nothing mediocre can have any value. Cherea is capable of distinguishing intermediate values: "I believe that some actions are more beautiful than others." "I believe," Caligula replies, "that they are all equal" (CL, pp. 78–79). For Cherea the source of that hierarchy of values is neither the true nor the good; the source is happiness. His wisdom is only a form of pragmatism; it blocks the logic of nihilism at the moment when that logic is about to render life impossible. Cherea, then, will defend the existing order without believing in it, in order to ensure the survival of men and of their mediocre happiness. The mind scandalized, "metaphysical anger" veers spontaneously toward the inhuman. Cherea has passed beyond that crisis, his revolt has become wisdom. He will kill the too intelligent emperor while at the same time understanding and even respecting his madness; Caligula has pushed further than he, to a point where he himself would never dare go, indeed to the very end toward which the evidence points.

The distance between Caligula and Cherea marks two ages in life, two opposing aspects of Camus, two periods in his reflection. When the play was produced in 1945, he was in harmony with Cherea's humanism and in his commentaries he puts the mad emperor on trial (*PL*, p. 1727). But in 1938, when he was conceiving the play, it was obviously Caligula's madness that interested him. It illustrated for him the delirious consequences of a coherent atheism such as he saw it outlined in Ivan Karamazov or Stavrogin. He used this drama, so to speak, as a proof by fire—the "fire" of the Absurd. By pushing them to their extremes, he rid himself of what was excessive and inhuman in his expectations and his denial.

Undoubtedly, Cherea has no response to give Caligula on the metaphysical level: the Absurd remains as repugnant as ever. But in the great precipice of nihilism he found a foothold: compassion. The dilemma that this play poses is the choice between truth and happiness. Because he could not choose, Camus gave birth to this tragedy where consciousness and life confront one another: how is it possible to "live at the pinnacle of this world's truth which is to have none at all"?

The Myth of Sisyphus—begun in 1938, published in 1943—has often been considered a manual of existentialist despair. It is not that at all. In this work Camus tried to channel the fury to live that drives a Caligula mad, to tame the fury, to make it operative in an absurd world. Paradoxical enterprise, since it meant maintaining at the same time two mutually exclusive truths: that of nihilism and that of happiness.

Camus does indeed place at the cornerstone the necessity for despair, and from this very despair he attempts to derive happiness. The anguish of Kafka's heroes comes from their being prey to hope; they are consumed by their nostalgia for paradise. Those who hope are sad. Camus learned from

Nietzsche that to cease hoping can be a deliverance. The tragic disappears immediately and life becomes radiant. Despair installs man in his own kingdom and, so to speak, gives him back to himself. "A world remains of which man is the sole master. What bound him was the illusion of another world" (MS, p. 158). If metaphysical anguish alienates, makes men mad (as we have seen with Caligula), clear-sightedness liberates: "Oppressive truths perish from being seen for what they are" (MS, p. 166). Sisyphus has taken the measure of the full extent of his suffering and, a slave victorious over his master, he has undertaken to be indifferent to it: "There is no destiny that cannot be surmounted through scorn" (MS, p. 166). Such is the theme of *The Myth of Sisyphus:* to become indifferent to "the essential" so as to liberate the fury to live and to be able, without mental reservation, to celebrate—according to Emmanuel Mounier's expression—the triumph of Dionysus amid the ruins of hope.

For this is without question a matter of intoxication. Since nothing is serious, since nothing has any absolute value, inanity must be compensated by impulsiveness, fragility by fervor. Like all nihilists, from Nietzsche to Gide, to Montherlant or to Malraux, Camus sought to soar over life, to toy with action, to take root nowhere. That is no doubt the only way to live when one is convinced of the existence of nothingness, but from it arises a shallow agitation that fixes one in inauthenticity. Curious consequence of the lucidity that henceforth keeps one from believing in what one does and from doing it out of enthusiasm! Nothing remains but to transform life into the outward appearances of living. Camus thus proposes four modes of existence that have the common characteristic of "sustaining he absurdity of the world" while imparting splendor to useless and meaningless acts.

First of all there is Don Juan. Thus Camus eulogizes, though not without a basic sadness, ephemeral loves. But how can the absurd man take love seriously without belying himself; would not fidelity to the "truth" of love oblige him to remain unfaithful? For love, like everything else, cannot have any depth. Our illusions are what lend it its seriousness. The absurd man cannot be a dupe; he knows that everything is only a deceitful surface. Therefore he seeks in quantity and diversity what a reality deprived of meaning cannot provide him. Such is the heavy tribute that lucidity imposes: the absurd man has put himself in a position of being unable to love . . .

That airborne lightness so dear to Nietzsche, that tight-rope dancer's bearing, Camus discovered in the actor, who is the perfect realization of the absurd man since he *plays* life while avoiding to live. In doing so, he imitates the great Universal Game, just as that tragic clown Caligula wanted to do.

Another simultaneously absurd and logical mode of conduct is that of the adventurer and the conqueror. This mode resembles that of Don Juan in that it always comes down to "giving color to the void" through agitation, speed, and diversity of experiences.

The artist is still another conqueror of the useless: "All of existence for a man turned away from the eternal is only an immense mime beneath the mask of the absurd. Creation is the great mime" (*MS*, p. 128). In creating, one plays out anew what was already no more than grimace—on the condition, of course, that one be perfectly aware of the vanity of what one creates.

In all of these modes of conduct what is striking is the decision to become light, in order to weigh no more on the surface of existence, in order to avoid encountering that other dimension of life which, by hypothesis, is only illusion—depth. As a result, no other alienation is worse than that of the supposedly "liberated" man. He lives outside himself, far from others, in the hostility of a universe that recedes from him, banished in an "exile without recourse since he is deprived of memories of a lost country or of hope of a Promised Land" (*MS*, p. 18). Everything happens as if the absence of God made man alien to everything. Mankind had, with religion, manufactured a world in his image and had "marked it with his seal." In dehumanizing it now, through the "death of God," he loses his hold on it. The world escapes us and becomes once more what it is: all that is most impenetrable to the mind. We lose everything, including our hold upon ourselves; so divisive is the strangeness of the Absurd that we cease to communicate with our own person: "The familiar yet disturbing brother that we find in our own photos, this again is the absurd . . . I shall forever be a stranger to myself" (*MS*, p. 29).

If *Le Mythe de Sisyphe* is in its profound intention a positive work that claims to open onto a new humanism, it must be admitted that it belies ceaselessly its own aims and its conclusion, and that the memory that it leaves is that of an unhappy consciousness seeking in vain to extract from its very misfortune a kind of grandeur. In fact, resentment is the dominant tone. Gabriel Marcel wondered, à propos of *L'Homme révolté*, "if the fact of not having anyone on whom to lay blame does not create in the soul of the rebel not only a disarray but what must be called an ulceration. The conscience in revolt becomes an ulcerated conscience

. . . a sincere atheist is almost inevitably exposed to experiencing a widespread resentment." Inveterate rancor, masked by an assumed attitude of indifference or a stoical pose. Nietzschean dynamism leads in Camus only to false solutions; neither Don Juan, nor the adventurer, nor the actor, nor the artist are the true witnesses of man. They succeed only in separating us from the essential. The event —the war—was going to snatch Camus from these reveries and impose upon him a humanism—perhaps the only atheist humanism that modern thought has succeeded in constructing.

Positive Values

How to reintroduce the human, that is to say, a hierarchy of values, into a world that the Absurd has flouted? To affirm certain values implies that the world is not absurd and that an *order* exists. That "recuperation" of order was Camus's great concern and in that concern his absurdist point of view distinguishes itself from the existentialist orthodoxy and merits truly the name of humanism. Camus experienced these values in himself, in his conscience as a man of honor filled with a sense of justice: "I saw scarcely any argument to oppose [to nihilism] except a violent inclination for justice which, in the end, seemed to me as little reasonable as the most sudden of passions" (*LA*, p. 240). Without a doubt, in an irrational world nothing is reasonable. However, the demands of justice are not a matter of reason, but an instinct as essential for man as his life instinct. "I chose justice in order to remain faithful to the Earth" (*LA*, p. 241). No metaphysical philosophy of the Absurd can resist when the voice of conscience has made itself heard. Camus did not ask himself any prelimi-

nary questions when, in 1937, it was a matter of conducting
his investigation of the famine in Kabylia, or when it was a
matter of calling the public's attention to the scandal of the
convict ship *La Martinière*, or when it was a question of
defending an agricultural agent subjected to persecution by
his superior.* Absurdism loses all its meaning when man
is victimized. There for this nihilist was a primary, indubitable truth out of which an ethic could be born amid the
ruins of hope and reason. This point of departure, which
recalls that of Rousseau and Kant, this categorical imperative, Camus drew out of his love of life. To love life is to
love and respect men and to avoid, even under the pretext
of their future happiness, inflicting suffering upon them:
"In the darkest depths of our nihilism I sought only reasons
to go beyond that nihilism. And not by way of virtue or a
rare elevation of the soul but out of instinctive fidelity to a
light in my native land where for thousands of years men
have learned to acclaim life even in its suffering" (*Eté*, p.
133). It was out of obedience to that spontaneous idealism
that he first joined the Communist Party in 1934 only to
leave it two years later, disappointed by the party's oppor-
tunism. Again out of idealism he joined the freemasons in
1936, drawn to that organization by an almost religious

* These incidents were treated in articles written by Camus
for *Alger-Républicain* in 1938–1939. "Ces hommes qu'on raie
de l'humanité," a description of the prisoners on the convict
ship *La Martinière*, appeared Dec. 1, 1938, pp. 1–2. The articles
on the arrest and trial of Michel Hodent, the agricultural
agent, appeared at intervals between Jan. 10 and Mar. 23, 1939.
The series on Kabylia, *Misère de la Kabylie*, comprises eleven
articles that appeared between June 5 and June 14, 1939 (a
number of these are reprinted in *Actuelles III*). See also,
Emmett Parker, *Albert Camus: The Artist in the Arena*. (Madison: University of Wisconsin Press, 1965) [trans. note].

atmosphere of fraternity and human solidarity. And again out of idealism he helped found a "true newspaper," one that was all the more scandalous in that it did not fear to tell the truth.*

But the war in Spain, the war of 1940, the Nazi invasion, the Resistance—such events would compel him to rethink this problem—no doubt an insurmountable one for an atheist—of the relations between absurdism and idealism. Henceforth Camus definitively understood that inviolate values do exist: "In the time of innocence I did not know that morality might exist. I know it now" (*Eté*, p. 146). In his *Lettres à un ami allemand* (*Letters to a German Friend* [1943–1944]), we witness a moving examination of conscience: "We long thought together," he wrote to his Nazi correspondent, "that the world had no superior reason and that we were stuck in an impasse. I still believe this in a certain way. But I have drawn from this other conclusions than those you spoke to me about then, and which you have been trying for so many years to force into the mainstream of History. I tell myself today that if I had really followed you in what you think, I ought to admit you are right in what you are doing. And that is so serious that I have to stop short at that point . . . You have never believed in the meaning of this world . . . you have concluded from this that man was nothing . . ." (*LA*, pp. 239–40). Camus was henceforth to oppose to this nihilism the affirmation of a human order, of a justice that is like a challenge to "universal injustice," and which constitutes the

* Camus collaborated in the founding of three newspapers: *Alger-Républicain*, *Soir-Républicain*, both in Algiers (1937–1939), and the post-Liberation Parisian daily, *Combat*, of which he was editor-in-chief from 1944 to 1947 [trans. note].

honor of man: without it there would no longer be any human life on earth. Humanism and struggle for justice are the same thing. To opt for man, that is to say for life, is to proclaim the existence of a good and thus escape from contingency, from despair—and from the cynicism that results from it. "If nothing had any meaning," he said to the Nazis, "you would be right. But there is something which still keeps its meaning" (*LA*, p. 228). This something is justice, which is the sublime creation of man and which he is "unique in conceiving." The Nazis betrayed men by consenting to disorder and by adding to it; Camus's revolt excludes such a connivance. A more radical antitheism, similar to Nietzsche's, delivers man from the nihilistic prison and hails in him the *creator of values*. These values will henceforth play the role of the absolute; the religion of man is substituted for pious or cynical resignation to Disorder. Thus in the darkest days of the Nazi Occupation, Camus discovered what hope can be: a kind of faith! "With equal energy, the truth wins over the lie," he wrote in 1944. Strange confidence in a final rationality of things! . . . Misfortune, by its very excess, snatched Camus from despair: "The war," he said in an admirable phrase, "united the dimensions of hope and the depths of revolt."*

We know how the events following the liberation of France in 1944 disappointed the generous hopes born in the misfortune of the Occupation years. Camus very quickly ran into progressist rationalism which, under the name History and a sense of History, restored ancient and inhuman Fatality. To the revolutionary rationale Camus opposed his concept of revolt, the same concept that earlier he had

* M. Onimus does not indicate the source (or sources) of these two remarks [trans. note].

opposed to chaos and natural evil. His fidelity to *life*, his respect for man, raised him up against those who were bent on imposing the reign of justice by any and all means, and it was in the name of the *sentiment* of justice that he was to combat the terrible doctrinaire ideologues of justice. Like Hercules wrestling with the Hydra, Camus saw reborn in another and, for him, entirely disconcerting new form that Evil that he had first identified with the natural world, that is to say with God, an Evil created this time by the hand of man and born out of the very passion for justice itself! 'After having long believed that it could struggle against God with all of humanity, the European mind perceives, then, that if it does not want to die it must also struggle against men. Rebels who, risen up against death, wished to build on the species a fierce immortality are frightened at being obliged to kill in their turn [. . .] The kingdom of grace has been vanquished but that of justice is being engulfed as well. Europe is dying from that disappointment," he proclaimed in 1951, at the end of *L'Homme révolté* (p. 346). In this outstanding book bursts forth the drama of atheistic humanism which, after having deserted God, finds itself in the presence of the bloody idols of reason. Camus was to break with the intellectuals of revolt and the "unconditionalists" of the Revolution. Of what use would even a victorious revolution be if it destroyed man's honor by enslaving him? It would betray its inspiration, which was precisely to enthrone that honor. Thus, less than ever in that domain could the end justify the means. This dilemma is posed by Camus's most forceful play: *Les Justes* (*The Just Assassins*), written in 1948 and produced the following year. Stepan is no longer anything but a fanatic, alienated by his ideal, become a stranger to all pity, all respect, all civilization. In contrast to him, Kaliayev is torn between

the contradictory demands of his political convictions and
his sense of responsibility. "I do not love life but justice,
which is above life," Stepan declares; to which Kaliayev
replies: "I chose to take part in the Revolution because I
love life" (LJ, p. 310). The antinomy between justice and
life, Camus's "cross," powerfully deepened his awareness of
Evil. The question is to know whether he allowed himself
"to be a criminal so that the Earth may be covered with
innocents." This problem is obviously not even posed for
the revolutionary who has, so to speak, only one dimension;
the militant resembles a robot. Camus, however, was en-
cumbered by the contradictions of ethical living; he discovered the impossibility of being pure. Man secretes evil even
in the exercise of what he calls virtue. "Perhaps evil is
everywhere," says Henri Perron in Les Mandarins,*
speaking of the Stalinist concentration camps. "If evil
was everywhere, innocence did not exist. Whatever he
might have done, he would have been wrong . . . If evil is
everywhere there is no way out, neither for humanity nor
for oneself. Must it come to our believing that?" Simone de
Beauvoir seized and expressed with exactness Camus's confusion: the discovery of the true dimension of Evil and of
human powerlessness. The plague infects man to such a
point that he cannot work for his own progress without
dirtying his hands: "We begin by wanting justice and we
end up by organizing a police force" (LJ, p. 365). Thus
revolutionaries, in order to be efficacious, see themselves
constrained to fall into the false position of which Marx
was so critical: their practical conduct becomes destructive
of the intentions that had caused them to act in the first
place, they posit values that they belie by their actions

* Simone de Beauvoir, Les Mandarins (Paris, 1954), p. 300

Camus had come to wonder if the passion for justice was not a nefarious passion and was not itself—strangely enough—part and parcel with nihilism. The "just" are madmen, strangers, and finally enemies—all the more dangerous because they carry with them the glory and the seductiveness of the ideal of justice and because men of our time hunger and thirst after that ideal. "For us who do not believe in God there must be *total* justice or we're stuck with despair" (*LJ*, p. 355). Thus the murderous rage of earthly justice is linked with atheism and the bloody face that History has taken on results from the blotting out of a divine image in the heavens. "All socialism is utopian and first of all scientific. Utopia replaces God with the future. It identifies, then, the future with morality; the only value is that which serves the future" (*HR*, p. 258). Such is the mechanism that makes of utopian socialism the continuator of the most constraining orthodoxies: "The sacrifices we grant to History inherit from those that we once granted to God." Man is sapped, emptied of his substance (of his happiness as well as his compassion, of what we call "human" sentiments), by the frenetic desire for an earthly order, a desire created by the disappearance of the divine order: "Having escaped from the prison of God, his first concern will be to construct the prison of History and Reason" (*HR*, p. 105). Thus reason reintroduces nihilism: "Here Prometheus' astonishing itinerary comes full cycle" (*HR*, p. 301). After having risen against the gods to effect mankind's deliverance, Prometheus, the engineer of humanity, becomes its oppressor. He symbolizes that kind of reason which "laying claim to the universal heaps up the mutilations of mankind."

How to snatch man away from the fascination that this new idol exercises over him?

By giving him back the taste for happiness and the sense of concrete realities. "We live amid terror because man has been completely bound over to History and because he can no longer turn toward that part of himself which is as valid as the historical part and which he rediscovers in confronting the beauty of the world and of human faces, because we live in the world of abstraction, that of offices and machines, of absolute ideas and of unmitigated messianism. We suffocate among men who think they are absolutely right, whether in their machines or in their ideas. And for all those who can live only amid dialogue and the friendship of men, this silence is the end of the world . . ." (*AI*, p. 332).

For Camus, in fact, humanism was summed up essentially in *dialogue* and in *compassion*, which are precisely what we lack the most.

Dialogue, that is to say, the liking and respect for the *other*, for his uniqueness, his autonomy, his opinions: there, for Camus, is the basis of a living humanism. In order to resist the monster of History, he found no other solution than to return—back beyond Christianity—to a pre-Christian wisdom, the wisdom of the Greeks. Christianity, and History which is its heir, project man outside himself, "disorbit" him by holding out hope in a palingenesis. Greek wisdom, however, did not envisage any kind of salvation. It led man back to himself and invited him to accept his own limits; it installed him in his kingdom. Like Socrates, Camus advocates that wise and candid ignorance "which attempts to deny nothing" (*AI*, 374), and which gives rise to reflection rather than scoffing at it. Like Pontius Pilate, he did not know the truth and withdrew to wash his hands. We must understand, nevertheless, what is positive in this secession, for it was to preserve the ideas of justice, freedom, and truth that Camus affected this skepticism in a world where, as Michaux put it, "ideas confront one another like goats" in a combat of hatred and death. Camus remained faithful to the "old humanism" and refused that new humanism to which Sartre was to rally, one that is "more realistic, more pessimistic, which gives a great place to violence and almost none to the ideas of justice, freedom, truth . . . there," Simone de Beauvoir adds, "is the only adequate morality in the present-day relationship of men among themselves."* Camus detested such a humanism on the ground that, in the end, it destroys man.

The sense of dialogue presupposes freedom and it is assuredly, in a human society, the essential value; a truth that one imposes is no longer a truth but a humiliation. Addressing himself to a group of Christians, Camus declared: "No man has the final word. We must place our reliance on a pluralistic doctrine and morality and create an intermediate universalism. Do Christians accept helping men define temporary values while momentarily abandoning recourse to superior values?" An absurd question perhaps when posed to men of religion, but one that testifies to a horror of ideological totalitarianism brutally manipulated by Marxism and to a concern for protecting man against all imperialisms of the mind.

Thus dialogue demands respect for "limits." This word often comes from Camus's pen from 1945 on. "Greek thought pushed nothing to the extreme," he tells us, "neither the sacred nor the rational [. . .] it *took everything into consideration* (*Eté*, p. 106). The revolutionary cries out, on the contrary, "there are no limits," the revolution has the right to everything (*LJ*, p. 338). Between extreme

* *Les Mandarins*, p. 470.

disorder and vicious order stands civilization, and civilization rests upon moderation. To civilize man is to reduce his ambitions and teach him the value of limits. Thus, in order to defend himself from the enterprises of an idealism that threatens "to disorbit the mind," Camus advocates equilibrium, harmony, respect for natural norms, and the overcoming through dialogue of mortal antagonisms. For him, as for Proudhon, justice is never anything but an "equilibration"; it is a justice in the process of "becoming," a *prudent* justice.

Dialogue presupposes a still more generous spirit than that of respect. It demands that one experience what Camus calls the inclination for mankind and what he sometimes calls "compassion" (*tendresse*). Doctrinaire militants who make history are hard; their faith and their hope render them sometimes pitiless. In their passion for transcendence they learn to hate nature and to detest men. The experience of the war and of the Resistance had an inverse effect on Camus: in the common misfortune, what could men do if not love one another? This theme is at the center of *La Peste*, the novel begun in 1942, published in 1947, and without doubt Camus's most beautiful book. The "redemption" of Tarrou, that solitary rebel so full of resentment, results from pity that will soon broaden into generosity, into self-sacrifice. There is a way out of the Absurd, then, a way very different from those artful dodges proposed in *Le Mythe de Sisyphe*. While remaining within the strict limits of an atheistic humanism, Camus at the same time rediscovered modes of conduct commensurate with acts of Charity. "There is no shame in being happy," declared Camus the sensualist of the 1930's (*N*, p. 22); "There can be shame in being happy all alone" (*LP*, p. 1837), Rambert admits after the plague reveals to him a self-centeredness that he had not at first been aware of. Here it is not a question of a principle, of a moral law, but of a very positive awareness. Camus had only scorn for the humanitarianism that "is nothing but a Christianity deprived of superior justification, which preserves the final causes while rejecting the primary cause" (*HR*, p. 104); thus we can rely on no system but rather on an entirely spontaneous *instinct* . . . life itself. When Rieux asks Tarrou if he knows a way capable of leading to peace of soul, Tarrou responds immediately: "Yes, sympathy" (*LP*, p. 1425). This is not quite Charity, rather more like friendship—that sentiment which Saint-Exupéry, during the same period, posited as the foundation of all civilization. In a dialogue imitated from Czselaw Milosz,* Camus placed Don Juan and a Franciscan monk face to face:

The Franciscan: You believe in nothing then, Don Juan?
Don Juan: Yes, Father, in three things.
Franciscan: May we know what they are?
Don Juan: I believe in courage, in the intellect, and in women.
Franciscan: Then we shall have to despair of you.
Don Juan: Yes, if one has to pity a happy man. Goodbye, Father.
Franciscan: I shall pray for you, Don Juan.
Don Juan: Thank you, Father. I see in that a form of courage.

* M. Onimus is mistaken in this attribution. The Don Juan dialogue was inspired by a *mystère* of the turn-of-the-century writer Oscar Vencelas de Lubicz-Milosz, *Miguel Mañara* (Grasset, 1912), a work to which Camus makes reference in *Le Mythe de Sisyphe* (Pléiade edition, p. 153). Czselaw Milosz is a contemporary French writer and critic [trans. note].

Franciscan: No, Don Juan, it is only a matter of two sentiments that you stubbornly persist in not recognizing: charity and love.

Don Juan: I recognize only compassion and generosity, which are the virile forms of those woman's virtues (*CN*, p. 215).

One is reminded of the dialogue between Polyeucte and Sévère.* Camus takes his place alongside Sévère, that is to say at the level of the lay saint who fills as completely as possible all the dimensions of his humanity while taking care not to go any further . . . Moreover, for Camus nihilism itself imparts value to what is human and exalts compassion: "How can we not understand," he had already written in *Le Mythe de Sisyphe*, "that in this vulnerable universe all that is human, and which is only that, takes on an ardent meaning. Upturned faces, threatened fraternity, men's strong and chaste friendship among themselves, these are the true riches since they are perishable" (*MS*, p. 121). In its broadest human sense, then, socialism establishes a fraternal bond among beings aware of the Absurd and deprived of a Father; it is the only means of eliminating God without sinking into despair (*HR*, p. 82). It makes the atrocious bearable: "Absurdity reigns and love saves us from it" (*CN*, p. 116). There is no love away from God, the Grand Duchess proclaims in *Les Justes*, and Kaliayev in his cell replies: "Yes, there is—love for the human crea-

---

* Presumably a reference to act 4, scenes 4 and 5, in which Polyeucte (in Corneille's play of the same name), faced with imminent martyrdom, gives his wife (Pauline) to his former rival (Sévère). The astonished Sévère replies that in Polyeucte's place he would have been satisfied with Pauline's love and physical presence alone [trans. note].

ture." "But," the Grand Duchess rejoins, "the human creature is abject. What else can one do but destroy him or
pardon him." The answer: "Die with him" (*LJ*, p. 375).
Thus is born, at the confines of atheism and nihilism, a
religion of humanity with its saints (Tarrou) and its mar-
tyrs (Kaliayev), in which devotion and abnegation expect
no reward and are accompanied by no prayer. By such
conduct men justify their existence and place Destiny, so to
speak, in the wrong: "We do not deserve so much injustice.
This is what our lives must prove."

Camus's humanism is an attempt to give a positive meaning to the rebel's *no*. In searching deeply into his revolt,
man perceives that he implicitly affirms certain values: "*I
rebel, therefore we are*" (*HR*, p. 36). Tarrou has reflected
a great deal, he has examined everything; he knows the
"whole of life," and this knowledge quietly and modestly
develops in him a warmth of heart, a need for generosity
unexpected in this lucid nihilist. As with ascetics and mystics, Camus becomes attached to terrestrial things only after
having questioned them. His humanism is a *point of return*
at which indifference and distance are still recognizable
even in the outpouring of sympathy itself. Thus revolt
"cannot do without a strange kind of love" (*HR*, p. 375).
But revolt is fundamental because it is "nostalgia for innocence and appeal to the being." There is in revolt a tragic
effort toward "recuperation of something that was lost."
Consequently, revolt, religious in its profound origins, is
atheistic and secular in the insurrectional violence of its
refusal and the haughty self-assurance of its affirmations.
Man exiled from innocence confers upon himself innocence and takes from that very effort his justification.

But what distinguishes Camus, and what endows him
with value in our eyes, is that he opposed "Promethean"

rationalism with all his strength; he did not cease to remind us that History is not everything and that values do exist "without which even a transformed world is not worth living in, without which even a new man will not be worth respecting . . . There is History," Camus states forcefully, "and *there is something else:* simple happiness, human passion, natural beauty" (*AI*, p. 368). Some may find such values poor indeed: sensual pleasure, estheticism, the reactions of a poet and lover. And it has to be admitted that they have little weight as against the demands and urgencies of History. But with these ingenuous words Camus emphasizes the existence within man of a soul that is not reducible to the Promethean will for progress and rationalization. This is what the existentialists and the Marxists cannot admit. This refusal to submit oneself to History caused Camus to waver—in their eyes—in a bourgeois and individualistic vision of the world. They must at all cost reduce man to Prometheus. But, Camus says, "a purely historical mode of thought is nihilist: it accepts totally the evil of history and in this stands in opposition to revolt" (*HR*, p. 356). A revolt faithful to itself will stand opposed *also* to what is inhuman in History. For this reason it rejects at one fell swoop Hegelianism, Marxism, and Nietzscheism which, each in its own way, worshiped either History or Destiny. In fusing revolt with History, Hegel dehumanized it. As for Nietzsche, Camus detested his "amor fati," his stoic submission to the Universal Law. For Camus *man is twofold* and one does not work toward his final realization but toward his destruction in wanting to satisfy his Promethean aspirations alone. Revolt thus rediscovers, in order to restore their worth, the most humble values of existence. In order to be total, revolt must be incarnated and Camus's greatness, in our eyes, lies in his having understood this and in his having proclaimed it.

A Conscience in Quest of its Judge

It has often been wondered what Clamence's strange confession in *La Chute* (published in May, 1956) signified in Camus's overall work and in his evolution. In fact, this disconcerting book, having appeared after a four-year silence, denotes a considerable progress in the consciousness and the experience of Evil. Until that time, Camus had not ceased to speak of happiness and of innocence as forms of fulfillment that are always worthy of attainment. To this end it was enough to cease being afraid and, in the manner of Kirillov, to accept death. In spite of his generation's climate of anguish, Camus remained the singer of happiness, of the joys of living and loving. Is not happiness more difficult and purer than heroism itself? To sum it up in a word, is it not more *human?* It comes nearest perfection because it crowns the victory of man over his destiny: "When it happens that I seek what is fundamental in myself, it is the desire for happiness that I find there." In *L'Etat de Siège (The State of Siege)*, the only sympathetic character, Diego—he will save the city—is a happy man, a man in love, an individualist. His very self-centeredness gives him the substance needed to struggle against the machinations of abstract collectivism. In happiness there is a strength that puts an end to the inhuman and which plants man more firmly upon the earth; without joy in living there is no humanism. "One day," Simone de Beauvoir relates, "Camus had said to us: 'Happiness exists, it means something . . . why refuse it . . . I find unfortunate that

shame we experience today in feeling ourselves happy.' "*
Happiness assumes an exceptional harmony between
awakening lucidity and the sensation that it feels, an assent
of the conscience that approves of itself with a sort of
innocence: "No one is a hypocrite in his pleasures" (LC, p.
1507). No more critical distance, no more irony or bad
faith; a totality is born within a man. There is something
sacred and primitive in happiness. If one could think for a
single instant that it does not exist, that it is a trap or a
fraud, then all humanism would collapse: "What comes
after death is futile." Perhaps! But to be able to affirm that,
one must have glimpsed on this earth a fullness, a perfection
of being that will serve to orient existence.

Now here is Clamence. A man who was happy: "I took
pleasure in my own nature and we all know that is happiness, though in order to appease one another we sometimes
go through the motions of condemning these pleasures by
calling them selfishness" (LC, p. 1483). Indeed, Clamence
was not in any way selfish: a sought-after lawyer, he represented the poor without recompense; he helped them, com-
forted them, consoled them. His happiness, moreover, had
that cheerful resonance only because it rested on the sense
of duty and the practice of virtue. To be sure, there was
nothing of the hero in him. But in the circumstances of the
plague he would doubtless have revealed the hero who slept
within him, exactly like Rambert and better than he, for
Rambert was at the outset nothing but selfish.

But there took effect in Clamence a strange work of
demystification that acted *against his own happiness*, revealing its illusoriness, the fraud. He became aware one

* Simone de Beauvoir, *La Force des choses* (Paris, 1963), p.
179.

night, while crossing the Pont Neuf, that he was nothing but a coward, and the cry of distress to which he had not had the courage to respond haunts him like a constant twinge of remorse. Caught in the very act of mediocrity, he came to take a new look at his own being and his own behavior; he found himself leprous and plague-ridden—the equal of all men. Then sarcasm and scorn took hold in him: self-scorn and, more serious yet, scorn for humanity in general.

It has been said that Clamence is the caricature of existentialism's moralists in quest of an impossible transparency and who, from the height of their scholastic Phariseeism, ceaselessly denounce the poses of others. Camus had been submitted to this kind of ordeal in 1952 during the quarrel over *L'Homme révolté*, and *La Chute* in this case would only have been an act of revenge. This interpretation cannot be set aside since the author himself lent support to it in an article in *Le Monde* (August 31, 1956). *La Chute*, Camus said, is "the picture of a little prophet, of which there are so many today. They announce nothing at all and find nothing better to do than to accuse others while accusing themselves . . ." Even before this, in an interview published in the *Gazette de Lauzanne* (March, 1954), Camus had criticized "those modern writers, and among them the atheist existentialists, who have denied the existence of God but have preserved the idea of original sin . . . they want to crush us with the sentiment of our own guilt." But, as in the case of Meursault, Sisyphus, or Caligula, and notwithstanding all the denials, the author inserted himself into his character. The sentiment of guilt is latent in Camus's earlier work; one reads in *L'Eté* that "in any case we are always guilty." *L'Envers et l'endroit*, from the preliminary essay (*L'Ironie*) to the last, is one long admission of guilt. "To a bad conscience confession is necessary. One's work is a confession." This notation dates from 1936.* From that time Camus's work owes its resonance to the fact that it is, in effect, a confession. Cottard, in *La Peste*, is unhinged by his bad conscience, and even before the outbreak of the epidemic he was already suffering from an internal plague: "I knew it before them," he says. Tarrou is a "heart rent asunder" in search of an impossible innocence (*LP*, p. 1236) and envious of the Oranais in their thoughtless positivism. "I learned this," he murmurs, "that we are all in the midst of the plague and I lost all peace" (*LP*, p. 1423). But finally, even in Tarrou's case, Evil seemed to come from outside man and to bestow an innocence. Clamence represents quite another matter: it is not only against Evil that he is led to rebel, it is against himself for Evil is *within* man. From *La Peste* to *La Chute* Evil moves, if one may say so, from God toward man, and it is man who henceforth finds himself under indictment. In *La Peste* Cottard still inspires only a sort of pity, but in *La Chute* sarcasm reigns; Clamence pardons nothing. He had seen himself forced to drain dry within himself the two sources of happiness—the pleasure of admiring and the pleasure of loving—and nothing now remains for him except to mock, and the only pleasure permitted him is criticism of others for the purpose, undoubtedly, of assuaging his self-criticism.

A character of this kind goes far beyond being a satire of the contemporary scene. Clamence bears witness to a sickness that is in the conscience, that is to say, in what is most noble and pure in man. Man is then irremediably wedded

---

* This entry in the *Carnets* (p. 15), the initial one, is not from 1936 but is dated "*Mai* 1935" [trans. note].

to his duplicity and without any hope of salvation. We are quite far from the arrogant humanism of Kirillov.

What happened then to Camus? Toasted, heaped with praise, admired by a whole youthful generation, he began, like his hero Jonas in *L'Exil et le royaume*, by accepting these praises. With his characteristic impetuosity he plunged into Parisian life. A great writer who in addition works in the theatre is exposed to a thousand temptations —and Camus was not one to resist the appeal of pleasure. It was a boisterous kind of life and, for one who had access to the wings offstage, an extremely free one. A disturbing, soon unbearable, contrast took hold between the idealism of his work and the disorder of his personal behavior. "He always returned," Simone de Beauvoir recounts, "to a theme that preoccupied him: one day the truth would have to be told. The fact is," she adds, "that with him there was a deeper division than in other writers between him and his work . . ."* The four years of silence that followed *L'Homme révolté* were years of fatigue, sickness, and relative sterility; a process of introspection began to occur. *La Chute* marks that metamorphosis; in the end, Camus could not avoid telling the truth . . .

It is in Paris that Clamence began to despise himself. It is under the skies of Amsterdam that he has taken up residence as a "judge-penitent," at the center of the concentric canals that recall the circles of Dante's *Inferno*. That is to say, he resides in the very core of Hell. So long as Camus lived in the sunlight of Algiers he could ignore sin, but in the countries of the north, in the plague-ridden world concentrated in the large cities, in the middle of stone and gray waters, on nocturnal bridges, in the opaque air and

* *La Force des choses*, p. 65.

dirty snow, far from life's wellsprings and far from nature, a part of his being began to drift far away from him.

Camus's great merit lies in his having consented to this confrontation, to that indictment of happiness, to this resounding and public penitence.

The idea of some form of guilt—personal or collective—is one of those sentiments of Christian origin that persists in the framework of atheistic humanism. One could say that the nostalgia for innocence becomes all the more throbbingly painful when God departs and good no longer has absolute support. Innocence is integrality. If man cannot be innocent there is for him then no hope at all of his existing fully, of his ever "realizing himself." "The idea most natural to man, one that comes to him naïvely from the depth of his nature, is the idea of his innocence" (*LC*, p. 1514). Now if that idea is a delusion, happiness is a lie: "Yes we have lost the light, the mornings, the holy innocence of him who pardons himself" (*LC*, p. 1548). If man cannot bestow pardon upon himself, who will grant it him? And how can we hope henceforth for the regeneration that makes life bearable? Guilt becomes exasperated before the emptiness of Heaven. Man deprived of his judge, in order to calm the irritation of his conscience now has recourse only to the public, to the stare of others. Clamence proclaims his fault and in so doing compromises others and puts them under an obligation to make a parallel confession. Perhaps a community of judges-penitent would come as near as it is possible to innocence? Men would reciprocally lighten each other of their respective burden of Evil by agreeing to bear it and thus we could all begin to breathe again . . . ? Alas! even that is impossible: "To become innocent it is not enough to accuse oneself" (*LC*, p. 1522). It is not even enough to extend condemnation to everyone and, so to speak, to dilute it (*LC*, p. 1541). This solution—which is Clamence's —leads only to a morbid masochism, to making of one's evil a sensual pleasure and, under the protection of public confession, to accepting one's real nature: "I allow myself everything . . . I have not changed my life. I continue to love myself and to use others. Only the confession of my faults permits me to begin anew more lightly and to take my pleasure twice: from my nature first and then from a delightful repentance" (*LC*, p. 1546). With what pitiless lucidity Camus probed the Tartufe that we all bear within us.

This sickness is congenital. It results from reflection: "After long research into myself I brought to light the profound duplicity of the human creature" (*LC*, p. 1516). Following in Sartre's footsteps, Camus affirms that the conscience cannot exist without bad faith. To be conscious is always more or less to take part in a spectacle. Camus always loved the theatre. In his daily actions he behaved like an actor, he never ceased acting, not to deceive but, on the contrary, in order to stand apart and to "empty illusions of their 'false seriousness.'" The theatre is the only place where one can be innocent because there one has deliberately planned to play a role and by so doing to reveal. Clamence, under the pretext of arrogating such an innocence, has become the mime, the juggler of his former happiness. He picks apart its fabric the way the dramatist dissects his characters. In general we play our role without even being aware that this is what we are doing. But the consciences of Camus and Clamence are too sensitive; they are too alert not to see themselves acting and to despise their own pantomime. Hence they mug their roles, extracting from them all the grotesque, indeed all the ignoble elements, and fling them as fodder to the public. Is man not always reduced to miming—even if it be miming his goodness—to playing a part in that vast comedy that is the universe of consciences? But for having proclaimed that such is the case, is he any the more innocent of miming?

The misfortune of which Sisyphus complained is nothing compared to the impossibility of finally being oneself, of being a transparent block . . . Having put on trial his epoch, History, injustices, the excessive demands we endure each day—having done all that, Camus seizes at last upon an essential evil for which the invention of the judge-penitent is a poor palliative: self-hatred, that hatred for which, according to the Catholic novelist Georges Bernanos, there is no pardon. In *Un Mauvais Rêve* (*A Bad Dream*), Bernanos probed "that foundation block of the soul, the very last one, that secret hatred of oneself that is at the utmost depth . . . probably of every life."* But Bernanos had, in order to become reconciled with himself, "that supernatural knowledge of oneself—of oneself in God—that is called faith."** He did not come to it easily and the natural horror persists beneath the humiliating acceptance imposed by that faith. "It is easier than one thinks to hate oneself," Bernanos writes. "Grace is to forget oneself. But if all pride were dead within us, the grace of graces would be to love oneself humbly, like any one of the suffering members of Jesus Christ."***

For the atheist armed only with his own witness and that of other men, there is no possible way out except to consent to deception. The intermediate solution, that of pardon, is forbidden to him, for man is too close to himself and too

* (Paris, 1951), p. 238.
** *Journal d'un curé de campagne* (Paris, 1936), p. 32.
*** *Journal* . . . , p. 321.

self-concerned to be able to forgive himself. He does not
have the right to do so.

Thus humiliated in his pride, man takes revenge in wan-
tonly destroying himself and in destroying all values. Clamence's nihilism is proportionate to his disappointment: the
collapse is total. "From the day that I became alerted . . . I
received every wound at one fell swoop and I lost my
strength in a single blow. The entire universe began to
laugh all around me" (LC, p. 1514). Hence the rage, the
hissing sarcasm, the restrained violence. Let us not be
dupes: this man is not a penitent but a witness for the
prosecution, and it is against men, all men, that he bears a
grudge for their being only what they are, for their flout-
ing of love, for their playing the comedy of being good, for
their being satisfied cowards and happy egoists. There he is,
Clamence, stuck in an odious confrontation, reduced to
destroying himself like Bernanos' Simone in *Un Mauvais
Rêve*. In the presence of the entire public that watches him
and that he summons, he is alone; no human word can
pluck him from his vertigo: "Ah, my friend! do you know
what he is, the solitary creature roaming about in the great
cities?" (LC, p. 1534). What a remark, and what light it
throws upon the anguish of him who wrote it!

To be rid of such anguish one must be able to make of
oneself a thing, to become a robot, to no longer have to do
anything but obey. Camus did not recoil before such consequences. When one thinks of the value he attached to
freedom, the condition for all dignity, one is frightened by
such lucidity. Developing the logic of his hero, Camus had
him express a scandalous nostalgia for servitude: "The essential is to be no longer free and to obey . . . So long live
the master, whatever he may be, in order to replace the law
of Heaven" (LC, p. 1543). Do not such words seem to im-

ply that, for lack of his judge, freedom is unacceptable to the conscious atheist and that he comes to wish for slavery? The taste for servitude is implied in the logic of a "world without judge where no one is innocent" (CL, p. 107). Happy slaves who have the good luck to be innocent! In the view of a man who is lucid and therefore conscious of his guilt, innocence becomes the most dangerous temptation, since it beckons him to a desperate regression that leads to the "happiness of stones"—to Meursault.

The desire for innocence and the sentiment of guilt engender such a hatred for life that one is seized by vertigo. Pride and horror have joined forces here. Of all that composed the grandeur of man there remains only the dull drunkenness of humiliation.

La Chute is decidedly a terrifying book. Clamence's logic and cold irony recall the similar qualities of Stavrogin, he too being incapable of living with his conscience.

From the religious point of view, the most Dostoevskian of Camus's heroes is also the most ambiguous. Did not Bishop Tihon tell Stavrogin that the sinner aware of his evil is at the last rung of the ladder, the one that precedes prayer and pardon? The last, the most difficult step to take. Clamence's drama consists in his being vainly in search of a judge: "Who would dare condemn me in a world without judge where no one is innocent?" (CL, p. 107). No condemnation? Then no pardon either! Man is alone with his sin and no savior is going to deliver him from it. For only a savior, one having power over sin, could in fact cure him: and that is why guilt finally forces him to his knees. Freud maintained in his celebrated pages on the subject that religion is constructed on this sentiment. A neurosis can result from the absence of punishment and the nostalgia for a sanction is such that it sometimes provokes suicide. Clamence tried to punish himself by abandoning his job, by withdrawing, like a hermit, into the tumult of Amsterdam, and—especially—by intoning his *mea culpa* before anyone who cared to listen. But is this enough? "One cannot die without having owned up to all his lies" (*LC*, p. 1519). This is the instinct for confession in its raw state. In the perspectives of atheism he comforts himself on the psychiatrist's couch: "Ah, my dear man, for whoever is alone, without a god and without a master, the weight of the days is terrible . . . There is no longer any father, any rule, one is free. Then one has to get along on one's own . . ." (*LC*, p. 1542). Salvation? The miraculous solution, the only satisfactory one, but in which, alas!, one cannot believe. "After all, it was a stroke of genius to say to us: 'You aren't any shining lights, all right, that's a fact. Ah well, we're not going to quibble about it! we're going to take care of that at a stroke, on the cross . . .' " (*LC*, p. 1532).

Clamence is obsessed by his sin. The young woman whom he did not have the courage to save haunts his memory: "It is too late," he keeps saying . . . But he adds at once: "Fortunately!" (*LC*, p. 1549). If that young woman could throw herself once more into the Seine and if he were by chance passing at that precise moment, if everything could be begun anew, redeemed, obliterated . . . what would happen? Clamence is lucid enough to know that nothing would happen, that he would quite simply repeat his act of cowardice. Because man is evil and because, if he could begin his acts anew, he would always perform them just as badly. Such is Clamence's pessimism. And we are still close to Augustine.

One can truly ask oneself, with the critic Marcel Arland, if in driving man to despair "this devil's advocate does not serve God's cause . . ."

4

A Great Unfulfilled Love

Anima naturaliter religiosa, the soul is naturally religious, says François Mauriac, speaking of Camus. Yes and no . . .

Yes, because of the need for the absolute and for innocence. Camus's protest is a revolt against the absence of God; it is the "lucid protest of a man cast up on a land whose splendor and light speak to him continually of a God who does not exist" (*N*, p. 81); it is the refusal to admit that the truth of this world is *not to have any* (*CN*, p. 187).

But to suppose for a moment that God exists, His aspect for Camus could not be that of a father; rather it is that of a tyrant or even a monster. By a terrible inversion God has become a stupid and destructive demon, a Shiva dancing on skulls: Evil personified.

If the mystery of Evil had such a hold on Camus's spirit it is because his point of departure was the pessimistic view of Christianity that he learned from Saint Augustine and Kierkegaard. Thus, rather than to the God incarnated so humanly in Christ, Camus was introduced to a distant God, a hidden God to be sought less through love than by a

miraculous faith (the result of grac̣
humiliation of the intellect. This Chrisṭ
historic crises and personal tragedies, dị
fended Camus's humanism. To Camus, the
nomenon was nothing more than a refusal to
human condition.

But how, after this, is one to construct a humạ
How is one to build on emptiness? How can a philosop̣
of negation be made to coexist with a positive wisdom?
Camus's works are moving for their vitality, their will to
live despite everything—to live even with emphatic happiness amid the wreckage of metaphysical thought. Incoherence is not always the mark of illogic; it may well come
from fidelity to the object. Camus's thought is contradictory only in its having refused to bury the contradictions
on which the rational atheist flounders. Camus has, in his
words, "woven with white and black threads a single cord
stretched to the breaking point" (*EE*, p. 156). The white
thread is the vital instinct, Nietzschean joy, Gidian fervor,
prolific freedom, cosmic ecstasy, and love. The black
thread is that which is revealed by an attentive consciousness: vanity, the emptiness of all things, and among these,
hope, the misery of the humiliated, the injustice and cruelty
of that History that men thought to have constructed in
opposition to Destiny. Camus thought he had found a reason for living in the tension to which he subjected that
cord, a tension in which pain is mixed with happiness. He
called the tension "revolt," and it is the only "honor" man
has left: it saves him from self-contempt and from hatred
for existence and thus gives him something that resembles an
ideal. Atheistic humanism draws upon an energy that is an
end in itself and that imparts to existence all the dignity it is
capable of.

This is not all. The fate of Nietzscheism shows the danger of these energies when they are not tempered by any trace of prudence. Camus—and in this lies his originality—strove to join to his sense of revolt the necessary wisdom, and to graft Greek moderation to modern excess. But is this not to weld two incompatible metals? A static vision of the world united with the impatient transcendancy inherited from Christianity and secularized by the moderns? Yet there is no other salvation, because hope becomes mortal when it is secularized in History. If it is true that God does not guide the world, one must avoid substituting "reason" for God because reason can be an enemy of life. And Camus returns to that fundamental virtue, prudence, without which atheistic humanism gives in to the temptations of idealism and destroys itself in a clash of fanaticisms.

This generous but composite humanism is a "vital minimum." It bears witness to a great crisis that has dispossessed us of our values and left us naked in the face of our condition.

In Camus, the illusions of humanism—whether Goethian, technocratic, or Marxist—were exposed with a peremptory lucidity. No alibi is left for the Absurd; decidedly it is all or nothing, God or nothingness. Since God is based upon fantasy, we have no choice but to make nothingness our abode and by our courage surmont the "injustice" fate has done us. This humanism is a "provisional morality" to save us from the maddening rationalizations engendered by atheism, just as Cherea provisionally saved Rome from the overly intelligent Caligula.

But no, life will *not* be "the better lived for not having any meaning" (*MS*, p. 76). Such paradoxes, far from excluding it, actually surround what is at the center of our experience: the need for salvation. "The desperate con-

frontation of human questioning and the world's silence"
(*HR*, p. 16) renders provisional forms of wisdom vain:
"One cannot live well, knowing that man is nothing and
that the face of God is terrifying" (*L'Etat de Siège*, p.
300). Trapped in nihilism between a fearsome God and a
concept of History become inhuman, Camus tried with
admirable honesty to find, in spite of everything, some
reasons and some principles for living. But where there is
no God, can there be a man? From Meursault to Clamence,
did Camus ever do more than to investigate blind alleys?
For us, this is the essential question. And if the answer is
doubtful, then we are left with Pascal's *Pensées* and St.
Augustine's *Confessions*.

Yes, Camus is truly the secularized son of Augustine and
Pascal. His "passionate disbelief" is no less irrational than
their belief was, since in each case human reason has no
grasp either of an irrational world or of a God whose
existence is discernible to the heart alone. Certainly, "truth
is mysterious, elusive, always to be conquered," but it is
especially inaccessible to those minds who at the outset
affirm their exile and imprison themselves in the Absurd.
Camus is the heir to a religious persuasion that, in order to
dedicate man to God, has ceased to give mankind his place
in the universe and has made him a stranger to the world, a
stranger to himself. Atheistic humanism that is based on
these principles is fragile, painful, and—as Gabriel Marcel
has said—"ulcerated."

Parting from these tragic premises Camus obviously
could not find God *in* the world, at the very core of the
world, like a supernatural center toward which all nature
converges and, in the forefront of nature, man. His thought
is non-cosmic and statically oriented: he had no sentient
awareness of a Becoming animated by the Spirit. He per-

ceived instead a stagnant universe, a benighted chaos where human folly blazes. Hence that fear of History and of the undertakings of History, hence that regression toward prudent and skeptical philosophies that date from a time when History had not been born.

The "demoniacal" god of whom Camus speaks is the terrible but logical consequence of a philosophy that sought to tear man from the world in order to give him to God instead of giving him to God while revealing to man the true dimensions of his human task and his responsibilities in a creation which in its entirety ascends toward its Creator. No more than he believed in God did Camus truly have faith in the world, for those two convictions—our faith in the world beyond and our worldly expectations—are intimately joined. He saw neither the past nor the future nor the continuity of a past that gives meaning to the future. His concentration on the present confronted him with impassible discontinuities and irreconcilable oppositions. His thought is a manifestation of that absurdism of Christian origin whose effect has been to reduce so many of the sincere to atheism. That great cosmic love that animated his adolescence and that made of him a poet and a mystic was unable to take root in a humanism wherein man is a stranger to the universe and has not the same meaning as it does. On rereading *Noces* and *L'Eté*, then, one may wonder if Camus's spiritual life was not, ultimately, that of a great unfulfilled love.

Texts

N.B.: All the texts reproduced are taken from the Pléiade editions of Camus's works. The translations are my own. The bracketed commentaries and footnotes are those of M. Onimus [trans. note].

1936

An Old People's Religion*

[*In this sketch, composed in 1936 and later incorporated in* L'Envers et L'Endroit *under the title* "L'Ironie," *Camus evokes his illiterate and superstitious grandmother who gave him in early childhood a deplorable idea of religion.*]**

Two years ago I knew an old woman. She was suffering

---

* The titles used here are not those of Camus.
** Camus's grandmother may well have imparted to him a "deplorable" idea of religion, but the woman evoked in this sketch was almost certainly not his grandmother. See note, p. 60 [trans. note].

from an illness of which she was quite sure she was going to
die. Her entire right side was paralyzed. Only half of her
was left in this world, while the other half had already
become a stranger to her. A busy talkative little old woman,
she had been reduced to silence and immobility. Alone for
long days on end, unlettered, lacking much sensitivity, her
entire life was oriented toward God. She believed in Him.
And the proof is that she had a rosary, a lead crucifix, and a
plaster statue of St. Joseph holding the Christ Child.

She did not really think that her illness was incurable,
but she maintained that it was so that people would take an
interest in her, beyond that leaving the whole matter to the
God she loved so poorly.

On that particular day someone was taking an interest in
her. He was a young man. (He believed that a truth existed, and he had found out elsewhere that this woman was
going to die without worrying about resolving this contradiction.) He had taken a real interest in the old woman's
problems. She had definitely sensed that. And that interest
was an unhoped-for boon for the sick woman. She told him
animatedly of her difficulties: she was at the end of her
days and one had certainly to make way for the young.
Was she bored? That was for sure. People didn't talk to
her. She was off in her corner, like a dog. It was better to
have it all over with. Because she would rather die than be a
burden to someone.

Her voice had become querulous. It was a voice one
hears in the market place, a haggling voice. However, this
young man understood. He was of the opinion nonetheless
that it was better to be a burden to others than to die. But
that only proved one thing: that, undoubtedly, he had
never been a burden to anyone. And he was saying in effect
to the old woman—because he had seen her rosary: "You

still have the good Lord." That was true. But even so, a person was still bored. If she happened to remain absorbed in prayer for any length of time, if her stare lost itself in some figure in the wall paper, her daughter used to say: "There she is praying again."

"What difference does it make to you?" the sick woman would say.

"It doesn't make any difference to me, but it begins to get on my nerves after a while."

And the old woman fell silent, fixing on her daughter a long stare filled with reproach.

The young man listened to all this with an immense, an unfathomable pain that constricted his chest. And the old woman would add: "She'll see, she will, when she's old. She also will need them."

One sensed this old woman, cut loose from everything except God, given over entirely to this final illness, virtuous out of necessity, too easily persuaded that the only thing she had left to her was indeed the only possession worthy of love, plunged finally, and with no hope of return, into the misery of man with his whole faith in God. But let the hope of life be reborn and God loses his hold against man's purely human concerns . . . (*L'Envers et l'Endroit, P/I*, pp. 15–16.)

1940

The Prisoner and the Chaplain

[*Meursault, who has just been condemned to death, receives a visit from the prison chaplain. This scene expresses*

his rebellion against all forms of religious thought, a nos-
talgic turning toward nature, the will to "purge himself of
all hope," his desperate attachment for the Earth. Meursault
refuses to let himself succumb to anguish.]

At this precise moment the chaplain entered. When I
saw him I gave a little start. He noticed it and told me not
to be afraid. I said to him that his visits usually came at
another time. This, he replied, was just a friendly visit that
had nothing to do with my appeal, about which he knew
nothing. Then he sat down on my cot and invited me to sit
near him. I refused. However, he seemed a very pleasant
sort.

He remained seated a moment, his forearms on his knees,
staring at his hands. They were slender and muscular; they
made me think of two quick small animals. He rubbed
them slowly, one against the other. Then he remained that
way, his head still lowered, for so long I had a momentary
impression that I had forgotten all about him.

He raised his head abruptly and looked me straight in the
face: "Why," he asked, "do you refuse to see me?" I
replied that I didn't believe in God. He wanted to know if I
was quite sure of that, and I told him that I didn't have to
bother my head about that point: it seemed to me a matter
of no importance. He then leaned back against the wall, his
hands lying flat on his thighs. Almost without seeming to
talk directly to me, he observed that people think they are
sure sometimes, while in reality they are not. I said nothing.
He looked at me and asked: "What do you think?" I said it
was possible. In any case, I was perhaps not too sure about
what truly interested me, but I was absolutely sure about
what did not interest me. And the fact of the matter was
that what he was saying did not interest me at all.

He looked away and, still without changing position, asked me if I was saying that out of complete despair. I explained to him that I was not in despair. I was merely afraid—which was natural enough. "God can help you then," he remarked. "All those I've known in your situation turned to Him." I acknowledged that it was their right to do so. That proved also that they had time to do so. As for me, I did not want to be helped, and I in fact did not have time to develop an interest in what simply did not interest me.

At this, his hands moved in a gesture of irritation, but he sat up and smoothed out the folds in his cassock. When he had finished this, he turned back to me addressing me as "my friend." It wasn't because I was a condemned man, he went on to say, that he was talking to me this way. In his opinion we were all condemned to death. But I interrupted and told him it was not the same thing, and, what's more, that could not in any case be a consolation. "Of course," he agreed. "But if you don't die today, you'll die some other day. And then the same question will arise. How will you meet that terrible test?" I replied that I'd meet it exactly as I was meeting it now.

Upon hearing this, he stood up and looked me straight in the eyes. That was a game I knew well. I would often amuse myself trying it on Emmanuel or Céleste and most often they would lower their eyes. I saw right away that the chaplain was an old hand at this game; his gaze never faltered. Nor did his voice falter when he said to me: "Have you then no hope at all and do you live with the idea that your death will be the end of everything?" "Yes," I replied.

Then he lowered his face and sat down again. He told me he was sorry for me. He viewed such an attitude as unbearable for a human being. For my part, I only felt how much he was beginning to bore me. I turned away, as he had earlier, and walked over to the spot beneath the cell window. I leaned my shoulder against the wall. Without really listening to him I heard him start to question me again. He spoke in a troubled, urgent tone of voice. I became aware that he was upset and I began to listen to him more attentively.

He declared his assurance that my appeal would be heard favorably, but I bore the weight of a sin I had to get rid of. According to him man's justice amounted to nothing and God's justice was everything. I pointed out that it was the former which had condemned me. He retorted that it had not, for all that, washed away my sin. I told him I didn't know what a "sin" was. I had simply learned that I was judged guilty of a criminal offense. I was guilty, I was paying for it; no one could ask anything more of me.

At this he got up again, and it occurred to me that in this narrow cell, if he wanted to move about, he had no choice: you had either to sit or stand up.

My eyes were fixed on the floor. He took a single step toward me, and stopped, as if he didn't dare to come closer. He looked at the sky through the bars. "You're mistaken, my son," he said. "There's more that can be asked of you. It will perhaps be asked of you."

"Oh? What?"

"You might be asked to see."

"To see what?"

The priest looked all round him and answered in a voice that seemed to me suddenly very tired: "All these stones ooze with suffering and sorrow. I know this. I have never looked at them without feeling pain. But from the bottom of my heart I know that the most wretched among you have seen a divine face rise out of their darkness. It's that face you are asked to see."

I reacted somewhat to this. I told him I had been staring at those walls for months. There was nothing or no one in the world I knew any better. Perhaps, a long time ago, I had sought a face there. But that face was the color of sunlight and burned with the flame of desire: Marie's face. I had sought it in vain. Now that was all over with. And, in any case, I had never seen anything surge forth from that sweating stone.

The chaplain looked at me with a sort of sadness. I was now completely back up against the wall and the daylight was flowing over my forehead. He spoke a few words I did not understand and asked me, very quickly, if I would let him embrace me. "No," I retorted. He turned away and moved toward the wall, over which he slowly passed his hand. "Do you then really love this Earth that much?" he murmured. I did not answer.

He remained quite a while with his back to me. His presence was beginning to oppress and irritate me. I was going to tell him to go, to leave me alone when he cried out suddenly in a kind of outburst, wheeling around to face me: "No, I cannot believe you. I am sure that you have at some time wished for another life." I replied that of course I had, but that meant no more than having wished to be rich, to swim extremely well, or to have a better shaped mouth. It all came down to the same thing. But he interrupted me and wanted to know how I envisioned that other life. At that, I shouted at him: "A life where I could recall this one," and in the same breath I told him I'd had enough of him. He still wanted to talk to me of God, but I started walking toward him, trying to explain for the last time that I had little time left. I did not want to waste it with God. He tried to change the subject, asking me why I called him "sir" and not "Father." That set me on edge, and I said to him that he was not my father: he was with all the others.

"No, my son," he said, placing his hand on my shoulder. "I'm with you. But you can't see it because your heart is blind. I shall pray for you."

Then, I don't know why, something burst inside me. I started yelling at the top of my lungs and I shouted insults at him and told him not to pray for me. I had grabbed him by the collar of his cassock. I unleashed upon him everything that was in the depths of my heart in surges alternating between joy and rage. He seemed so sure, did he not? Yet not one of his certainties was worth a single hair on a woman's head. He wasn't even sure of being alive since he lived like a man already dead. I might seem to be empty handed. But I was sure of myself, sure of everything, surer than he, sure of my being alive and of the death that was bound to come. True, I had nothing but that. But at least I had hold of that truth just as it had hold of me. I had been right, I was still right, I was always right. I had chosen to live in a certain way, and I might have chosen to live quite another way. I had committed this deed and I had not committed that one. I had not done this particular thing while I had done something else. So what? It was as if I had been waiting all the time for that minute, that early dawn when I would be justified. Nothing, nothing had any importance, and I knew quite well why. He, too, knew why. From the depths of my future, during all that absurd life I had led up to now, an almost imperceptible breath of air rose to meet me from across the years that had not yet come and that breath of air, in passing, had rendered absolutely equal everything that anyone had ever proposed to me.

What were they to me, the deaths of others, a mother's love; what were they to me either, his God, the lives others choose, the destinies they pick out for themselves, since a single destiny was to pick me out, and along with me billions of privileged people who, like him, called themselves my brothers. Did he understand that? Every human being was privileged. There were none but privileged people. The others, too, would be condemned to die one day. He, too, would be condemned . . . I was nearly out of breath from shouting like that. But the chaplain was already being yanked out of my hands and the guards were threatening me. He, however, calmed them and looked at me for a moment in silence. His eyes were filled with tears. He turned around and quickly vanished from sight. (*L'Etranger, P/I,* pp. 1205–10.)

1943

Faith: A Gratuitous Choice

[*This text was written in 1943 after a rereading of Jean Guitton's* Portrait de Monsieur Pouget, *published in a review before the war. Camus had made extensive use of Guitton's thesis on* Le Temps et l'Eternité chez Plotin et Saint Augustin *(Time and Eternity in Plotinus and Saint Augustine) when he was writing his own thesis. The character of M. Pouget, viewed through Guitton's account, seems to have touched Camus by his modesty and loyalty. For him, M. Pouget is one of the "chosen," a modern "guru" and Guitton's work an "honest book." "Ah!" he was to say later to Guitton, "If all Christians were like your M. Pouget" (La Table ronde, February, 1960).*

In this text will be found an echo of the Kierkegaardian idea of faith as an entirely gratuitous and irrational choice. The intellect has no place in this domain. Consequently, unbelief is, for its part, as irrational as faith.]

All M. Pouget's effort seemed to lie in finding the middle road between blind faith and completely rational faith. He did not wish to uphold what could not be supported, to defend in the Scriptures ambitions they never had. M. Pouget threw all the ballast overboard . . . For him it was a matter of clearing out the brambles, of discerning an irreproachable minimum in the sacred texts, and of demonstrating that this minimum sufficed to prove the truths of faith. M. Pouget noted, for example, that we demand of the Scriptures a historical accuracy that no one would think of requiring of historians of Antiquity and the Middle Ages. One must deal, however, with the particular mentality of each age and with sudden changes in moral climate down through the centuries. And one must distinguish carefully in the Scriptures what is due to divine inspiration and what is owing to the mentality of a given epoch . . . God has scaled His revelations to the capacity of His creature. The illumination of divine light is too bright for human eyes and revelation must be graduated. "God is an educator," M. Pouget said . . . History is the succession of divine maneuvers designed to open up the blind human heart to the light of truth. Consequently one must seize revelation in its development, in its stubborn effort to free itself from successive layers of secular prejudices. The historical conscience is sacred . . .

These principles of minimum, of mentality, and of development are at the basis of M. Pouget's method, which does not grasp the problem by its very root, it is true. The root is the problem of Being, and M. Pouget seemed to mistrust metaphysics. In any case, the intellectual respect that his undertaking inspires obliges the commentator to remain within the framework chosen by the author. Within this framework, however, that method bares its flank to a very large objection. It risks, in fact, making of mentality the empty pocket of exegesis. Everything that contradicts faith boils down to mentality. Actual discussion of the question is elided . . .

On the other hand, one is more at ease in pointing out what appears to be of inestimable value in M. Pouget's reflections: the fact that they leave the problem of faith intact. Let us be clear. Is it necessary to say it? For M. Pouget himself the question never arises. But every exegisis supposes its unbelievers. Like Pascal's *Pensées*, M. Pouget's thought has an unstated aim: it is apologetic. But his method does not seek to accomplish conviction immediately. That is the work of grace. M. Pouget's critique was negative and preparatory. It aimed at showing that the inspired Scriptures present nothing that truly conflicts with common sense. The divine texts cannot be obstacles on the road to faith. They are, on the contrary, sure guides. "One does not derive faith from all this," M. Pouget said, "for *that is impossible;* but one finds sufficient reasons for believing." Thus, insofar as the intellect is concerned, such a modest and generous method leaves the question of faith intact. The choice remains entirely open; it is restored to its proper place.

For a hundred years in fact people have over-confused matters of faith and science.[1] A more flexible examination

[1] In fact, contemporary disbelief is not based any longer on the contradictions of science as it was at the end of the last century. It denies science and religion equally. The skepticism

of the question, on the contrary, renders total liberty to both Christians and unbelievers. The former no longer try to "demonstrate" revelation and the latter no longer use the fantastic genealogies of the Bible as a source of argument. The problem of faith does not repose amid vain quibblings. By the application of common sense M. Pouget gives back to grace its prestige. He returns everything here to its proper place, the only means of advancing the mind. These are the true merits of a method such as his. And these merits, for all their discreetness, are inestimable to the extent that they make one overlook the astonishing attitude that for three centuries kept Copernicus and Galileo on the Index or which raised up as a symbol of divinity the smallest comma in the Bible. ("Portrait d'un élu," *PL/II*, pp. 1599–1602.)

1946

Christian Pessimism

[*At the Dominican monastery of Latour-Maubourg, Camus, invited by Father Maydieu, explains himself, before a Catholic audience on the question of his pessimism. This text shows the persistent influence of Augustinian thought on Camus.*]

By what right may a Christian or a Marxist accuse me, for example, of pessimism. It is not I who invented human suffering, nor the terrible formulas of divine malediction. It

of reason is no longer opposed to the miraculous, but rather passionate disbelief. [This footnote is Camus's own (trans. note).]

is not I who loudly proclaimed that *Nemo bonus,** nor the damnation of unbaptized children. It is not I who said that man was incapable of saving himself all alone, and that from the depths of his degradation he had no hope other than in God's grace. As for Marxism's famous optimism: No one has yet gone so far in their mistrust of mankind. And, finally, the economic fatalism of their universe looms as something more terrible than divine capriciousness.

Christians and Communists will say to me that their optimism is more long-range, that it is superior to everything else and that God or History, depending on the case, are the satisfying ends of their dialectic. I might follow the same reasoning. If Christianity is pessimistic with regard to man, it is optimistic with regard to human destiny. Very well: I shall say that, pessimistic with regard to human destiny, I am optimistic with regard to man. And not in the name of a humanism that has always seemed to me wanting, but in the name of an unknowingness that tries to deny nothing.

All that indicates then that the words pessimism and optimism need to be more clearly defined and that, while waiting until this can be done, we must recognize what brings us together rather than what separates us. (*Actuelles I, PL/II*, pp. 373–74.)

1947

Father Paneloux's First Sermon

[*The plague begins to wreak its devastation. The Jesuit, Father Paneloux, has not yet encountered Evil. He speaks*

* See note, p. 82 [trans. note].

of it with facility, following a well-known apologetic, as God's punishment, a means of leading men back by way of "that exquisite light of eternity that lies at the depths of all suffering."]

"If today the plague holds you in its sight, it is because the time has come for reflection. The just can have no fear of this, but the wicked have reason to tremble. In the immense threshing-house of the universe, the implacable flail shall beat the human grain until the chaff is separated from the wheat. There will be more chaff than wheat, more called than chosen, and that great misfortune was not God's wish. This world has trafficked too long with evil, it has relied too long upon God's divine mercy. Repentance filled all needs, everything was permitted. And each man felt himself quite up to the task of repentance. At the right time one would assuredly yield oneself up to it. From there on the easiest thing was to let oneself go; divine mercy would do the rest. Well, that could not endure. God, who for so long a time turned upon the men of this city the divine face of pity, tired of waiting, disappointed in his eternal hope, has just turned away his eyes. Deprived of God's holy light, we find ourselves long since in the deep shadows of the plague."

In the hall someone snorted, like an impatient horse. After a short pause the priest continued, his voice lower: "We read in the *Lives of the Saints* of Jean de Voragine that in the time of King Umberto, in Lombardy, Italy was laid to waste by a plague so violent that the number of the living barely sufficed to bury the dead; and that plague was especially rampant in Rome and Padua. And a good angel appeared for all to see; he gave orders to the evil angel who bore a hunting spear and commanded him to strike the

houses; and for every blow a house received, so many were
there of the dead who came forth from it."

Here Paneloux extended both arms toward the cathedral
square, as if he were pointing to something behind the
moving curtain of falling rain: "My brethren," he said with
force, "it is that same death-hunt that rides today in our
streets. Do you see him, that angel of the plague, beautiful
as Lucifer and luminous as evil itself, risen up above your
rooftops, his right hand bearing the reddened spear head-
high, his left hand pointing out one of your houses. At this
very instant, perhaps, his finger is lifted in the direction of
your door; the spear resounds against the wood; at this very
moment the plague is entering your home, sitting in your
room and awaiting your return. It is there, patient and
watchful, as certain as the very order of this world. That
hand which it will hold out to you, no power on earth, not
even—and know this well—not even vain human science,
can help you escape it. And flailed upon the bloody thresh-
ing-floor of suffering, you shall be tossed aside with the
chaff . . .

"Long ago, the Christians of Abyssinia saw in the plague
an effective means, sent by God, of gaining eternal life.
Those who were not touched by it rolled themselves in the
sheets of the plague victims so as to be certain of death.
Undoubtedly that furious desire for salvation is not com-
mendable. It is the mark of a regrettable urgency very close
to pride. One must not be in a greater hurry than God, and
anything that seeks to precipitate the immutable order He
has ordained for all time leads to heresy. But, at least, that
example holds its lesson. To our more enlightened minds it
reveals only that exquisite eternal light which lies at the
depths of all suffering. That light illuminates the twilit
paths that lead toward deliverance. It is a manifestation of

the divine will which, without ever failing, transforms evil into good. Today once more, amid this processional of death, anguish, and outcries, it leads us toward the all-encompassing silence and the meaning of all life. There, my brethren, is the immense consolation I wanted to bring to you so that it might not be solely words of chastisement that you carry away from here, but also a divine message of solace." (*La Peste, P/I*, pp. 1294–97.)

1947

Death of a Child

[*A crucial episode. Father Paneloux who has just assisted at the long death agony of a little boy confronts an unbeliever, Dr. Rieux, who has been horrified by this spectacle.*]

. . . His mouth open, but empty of sound, the child lay in the hollow of the disordered bedclothes, suddenly become very small, traces of tears on his face.

Paneloux approached the bed; his hands made the gestures of benediction. Then he gathered up his cassock and left by way of the center aisle.

"Must we begin all over again?" [*] Tarrou asked Castel. The old physician shook his head.

"Maybe," he said with a tight smile. "After all, he held out a long time."

But Rieux was already leaving the room, walking so

[* Allusion to the ineffectiveness of a serum that Dr. Castel had just developed.]

rapidly and with such an air about him that when he passed Paneloux, the latter reached out to stop him.

"Doctor Rieux . . . ," he said to him.

In one swift angry movement, Rieux turned around and violently hurled in the priest's face: "Ah! That one in there, he at least was innocent, even you can't deny that!"

Then he wheeled around and, passing through the doors of the schoolroom ahead of Paneloux, walked over to the far side of the school courtyard. He sat down on a bench among the dusty little trees and wiped the sweat that was already running down into his eyes. He wanted to cry out again so that the violent knot that clutched his entrails might at last be loosened. The heat sifted down through the branches of the ficuses. The blue morning sky was being rapidly obscured behind a whitish haze that made the air even more stifling. Rieux sank down onto his bench. He stared at the branches and the sky beyond, beginning to breathe more normally, overcoming his fatigue little by little.

"Why did you speak to me so angrily?" asked a voice behind him. "For me too, what happened was an unbearable spectacle."

Rieux turned toward Paneloux: "That's quite true," he said. "Forgive me. But exhaustion is a form of madness. And there are times in this city when I no longer feel anything except my sense of revolt."

"I understand," Paneloux murmured. "What has happened is revolting because it goes beyond our ability to understand. But perhaps we ought to love that which we cannot understand."

Rieux straightened up suddenly. He looked at Paneloux with all the strength and passionate feeling he was capable of summoning, and shook his head.

"No, Father," he replied. "I have come to a different concept of love. And I shall refuse until the death to love this creation where children are tortured."

A stricken shadow passed over Paneloux's face.

"Ah! Doctor," he said sadly, "I have just come to understand that which we call grace."

But Rieux had sunk back down onto his bench. Out of the depths of his fatigue which had swept back over him, he replied, more gently this time:

"It is what I do not have, I know. But I don't want to discuss that with you. We are working together for something that unites us over and beyond blasphemies and prayers. That alone is important."

Paneloux sat down next to Rieux. He seemed deeply touched.

"Yes," he said, "yes, you too are working for man's salvation."

Rieux attempted to smile.

"Man's salvation is too big a word for me. I don't go so far as that. His health is what interests me, his health first of all . . ." (*La Peste, P/I*, p. 1394.)

1947

Father Paneloux's Second Sermon

[*Overwhelmed by the child's death, Paneloux has reflected. His reply henceforth is that of Job: we must choose between faith and nothingness. And if one chooses faith, he must silence his protest and bow down in acceptance. This is a passage of great spiritual import, in which*

Camus shows how far he went toward a profound understanding of religion's value.]

[Paneloux] spoke in a gentler and more reflective tone of voice than he had the first time, and on several occasions the persons present noted a certain hesitation in his delivery. Still more strange, he was no longer saying "you" but "we". . . .

Rieux understood somewhat distractedly that, according to the priest, there was nothing to explain. The Doctor's attention became fixed, however, when Paneloux said emphatically that there were things we could explain with respect to God and others we could not. Certainly good and evil existed, and, generally speaking, we could easily explain what set them apart from one another. But the difficulty lay within the very core of evil itself. There was, for example, apparently necessary evil and apparently useless evil; there was Don Juan plunged into Hell on the one hand and a child's death on the other. For if it were just that the libertine be struck down, the child's suffering was incomprehensible. And, in truth, there was nothing on earth more important than a child's suffering and the horror attendant upon that suffering, nothing more important than the explanation that had to be found for it. In all other aspects of human life, God made things easy for us to understand, and up to the point that He did this, religious faith had little merit. On this question, however, He had placed us before a blank wall. We found ourselves thus under the battlements of the plague and in their mortal shadow we had to seek out what benefit was there for us. Father Paneloux refused even to accept the easy means at hand which might permit him to scale the wall. It would

have been easy for him to say that the eternal joys awaiting the child could compensate his suffering, but, in truth,
it was beyond his capacity to say that. Who could in fact
state with certainty that an eternity of any kind of joy
could compensate for even an instant of human pain? Assuredly not a Christian whose Lord had felt the deepest
human pain in his soul. No, Father Paneloux would stay at
the foot of the wall, faithful to that brutal dismemberment
whose symbol was the cross, and face to face with the
child's suffering. And he would say without fear to those
who were listening to him that day: "My brethren, the
moment has come. We must accept everything or deny
everything. And who now among you would dare to deny
everything?"

Rieux barely had time to reflect that the priest was skirt-
ing heresy; he was already continuing with great force, and
going on to declare that that injunction, that imperative
demand, was the Christian's great benefit. It was his virtue,
as well. Father Paneloux knew that the element of excess in
the virtue of which he was going to speak would shock
many souls accustomed to more indulgent and more traditional moral lessons. But religion under the aegis of the
plague could not be an ordinary, everyday religion, and if
God could permit and even desire for us peace and joy of
soul in happy times, it was His wish that, before excess of
misfortune, the soul's reaction be excessive. God today
favored His creatures by placing them in the midst of
misfortune of such magnitude that they had of necessity to
rediscover and assume the highest of virtues: that born of
choosing between All or Nothing . . .

Paneloux stopped, and Rieux heard more clearly now,
under the heavy doors of the cathedral, the wind's com-
plaint, which seemed to have redoubled outside. The next

instant the priest was saying that the virtue of total acceptance of which he spoke could not be understood in the
restricted sense we ordinarily give it, that it was not a
matter of resignation, nor even of hard-to-achieve humility.
It was indeed a matter of humiliation, but a form of humiliation to which the humbled consented. Certainly, a child's
suffering was a humiliation for both heart and spirit. But
that was why it must be entered into; that was why, and
Paneloux assured his listeners that what he was going to say
was not easy to say, we had to wish it: because God wished
it. Thus the Christian alone would hold nothing back and,
all escape routes blocked off, would go straight to the heart
of the essential choice. He would choose to accept everything to avoid being reduced to denying everything. And
like the good, simple women who, in our city's churches at
that very moment, having learned that the buboes which
formed on the plague victim's body were the body's natural
way of rejecting the infection, were praying for their loved
ones, saying: "Please, my God, let him have buboes," the
true Christian would be able to abandon himself to the
divine will, incomprehensible though it be. One could not
say, "That I understand, but this is beyond acceptance";
we had to go straight to the heart of whatever beyond
acceptance was offered us, precisely in order that we might
make our choice. The suffering of children was our bitter
bread, but without this bread our souls would die of their
spiritual hunger.

The subdued shuffling that generally accompanied Father Paneloux's pauses had barely begun when, unexpect-
edly, the orator took up again in a strong voice. Putting
himself momentarily in the place of his listeners he asked
what, in the end, was the course of action to follow. He
was quite sure that many were going to pronounce the

frightful word, "fatalism." Very well, then, he would not balk at that term, if he were permitted only to affix to it the adjective "active". . .

He did not mean that we should reject all precautions which were the rational order that a society introduced into the disorder brought by a scourge. We must not listen to those moralizers who said we had to fall on our knees and surrender entirely. We needed only to begin marching forward, into the shadow of the wall, feeling our way, and trying to do what was good. But beyond that, we must go no farther, and without question leave the rest in God's hands—even the death of children—and do this without seeking any personal recourse . . .

"My brethren," Paneloux said at last, announcing that he was concluding, "God's love is a difficult love. It assumes complete self-surrender and disregard for our own persons. But He alone may wipe out the suffering and death of children—He alone in any case has made them necessary —because it is impossible for us to understand them, and because we can not do other than wish for them. There is the hard lesson I wanted to share with you. There is the image of faith, cruel in the eyes of men, decisive in the eyes of God, which we must come to. We must seek to be equal to this terrible image. Upon that summit, everything shall be confounded and all things shall become equal; the truth shall spring forth out of apparent injustice. It is thus that, in many churches in southern France, victims cut down by the plague have slept for centuries beneath the choirs' paving-stones while priests preach above their tombs, and the spirit which their words spread abroad springs forth out of that sleeping dust to which children, too, have after all contributed". . .

To Rieux, who gave him an account of Paneloux's

words, Tarrou said that he had once known a priest who had lost his faith during the war when he uncovered the face of a youth whose face was bashed in.

"Paneloux is right," Tarrou said. "When innocence has its face bashed in, a Christian must lose his faith or accept having his own face bashed in. Paneloux does not want to lose his faith; he will go all the way. That's what he wanted to say." (*La Peste, P/I*, pp. 1399–1403.)

Revolt and the Sacred

The Inca or the [Hindu] pariahs do not raise the problem of revolt, because it has been answered for them in a tradition before they have had a chance to raise it, the response being the sacred. If, in the sacred world, we do not find the problem of revolt, it is because in truth there is no real problematical concern, all answers being given at one and the same time. Metaphysics is replaced by mythology. There is no longer any questioning, there are only eternal answers and elaborations, which can then be metaphysical. But before man enters into the domain of the sacred, and for him to be able to enter it as well, or from the moment he leaves it, and for him to be able to leave it as well, comes questioning and revolt. The rebel is man historically situated before or after the reign of the sacred, who turns toward demanding a human order where all responses are human, that is to say, rationally formulated. From that moment forward, every question, every word is an act of revolt, while in the world of the sacred, every word is an act of thanksgiving. It would be possible to show also that for a human mind there are only two possible universes, that of the sacred (or, to use Christian terminology, of

grace) and that of revolt. The death of either one coincides
with the birth of the other, although that birth can manifest
itself in disconcerting forms. Here again we rediscover the
All-or-Nothing concept. The contemporaneity of the
problem of revolt lies only in the fact that in our day whole
societies have decided to place themselves outside the domain of the sacred. We are now living a deconsecrated
history. Man, to be sure, cannot be reduced to a mere force
of insurrection. But the history of today, through its con-
testations, forces us to say that revolt is one of man's essential dimensions. It is our historical reality. Unless we turn
away from reality, we must find in it our values. Can we,
having left the world of the sacred and its absolute values
far behind us, find rules for action? Such is the question
revolt poses. (*L'Homme révolté, PL/II*, pp. 430–31.)

1951

Metaphysical Revolt

[*Here is the definition of modern "antitheism." Camus
does not claim as his own a sentiment whose historian he
was to become. He only reveals at its point of origin a state
of revolt that constitutes, in his eyes, the essence and the
dignity of man.*]

Metaphysical revolt is the gesture by which a man rises
up against his condition and the whole of creation. It is
metaphysical because it questions the ultimate ends of both
man and creation. The slave protests against conditions
imposed upon him by the very nature of his state; the
metaphysical rebel protests against the conditions imposed

upon him by the very fact of being a man. The rebellious
slave affirms that there is something in him which does not
accept the way in which his master treats him; the metaphysical rebel declares himself baffled and frustrated in his
very being by creation. For each of them this is not merely
a matter of a negation pure and simple. In both cases, in
fact, we can discern a value judgment in the name of which
the rebel withholds his approval of the condition that is his.

The slave risen in revolt against his master does not
concern himself, we must be sure to note, with denying
that master in his capacity as a being. He denies him in his
capacity as a master. He denies that the latter has the right
to deny him, the slave, in his capacity as a being whose very
existence supposes certain demands. The master is held
forfeit to the very extent that he does not respond to those
demands which he ignores. If men cannot refer to a set of
common values, recognized by each and everyone, then
man becomes incomprehensible to man. The rebel demands
that these values be clearly recognized in himself because
he suspects or knows that, without this principle, disorder
and crime would reign over the world. The sentiment of
revolt is born in him as a demand for clarity and unity. The
most elementary form of rebellion expresses, paradoxically,
an aspiration toward order.

This description fits the metaphysical rebel line for line.
The latter rises up over a shattered world to demand unity
within it. He opposes the principle of justice that lies
within him to the principle of injustice that he sees at work
in the world. Thus, at the outset, he wants nothing more
than to resolve that contradiction, to install the unitary
reign of justice if he is able, or of injustice if he is pushed to
the extreme. In the meantime, he denounces the contradiction. Protesting against the human condition for its lack of

potential fulfillment—due to death—and its lack of coher-
ence—due to evil—metaphysical revolt is the protest, moti-
vated by desire for a happy unity, against the suffering
inherent in living and dying. If the criminal death sentence
universalized defines man's condition, revolt, in one sense, is
coincidental to it. At the same time he denies his mortal
condition, the rebel refuses to recognize the power that
forces him to live in that condition. The metaphysical
rebel, then, is most assuredly not an atheist, as one might
think, but he is by force a blasphemer. Simply stated, he
blasphemes first of all in the name of order, denouncing in
God the supreme scandal and the progenitor of death . . .

The history of metaphysical revolt cannot be co-related
with that of atheism. From a certain point of view it is
actually a part of the contemporary history of religious
sentiment. The rebel defies rather than denies. In the first
stages at least, he does not suppress God; he simply speaks
to Him as equal to equal. But this is not a polite dialogue. It
is a polemic animated by the desire to conquer. The slave
begins by claiming justice and ends up wanting kinghood.
He must dominate in his turn. The uprising against his
condition is organized into an over-zealous expedition
against heaven with the intent of bringing back a prisoner-
king whose fall will be proclaimed first, and his death
sentence next. Human rebellion culminates in metaphysical
revolution. It progresses from outward display to deeds,
from the dandy to the revolutionary. The throne of God
overturned, the rebel will come to see that it is now his
place to create with his own hands the justice, order, and
unity that he vainly sought in his own condition, and
thereby to justify the divine downfall. Then a desperate
effort will be launched to found, through criminal acts if
necessary, the empire of men. This will not come about

without terrible consequences, only a few of which we are yet aware. But these consequences are not due to revolt itself, or, at least, they only come to the fore to the extent that the rebel forgets his origins, grows tired of the arduous tension between assent and denial, and abandons himself finally to total negation or total submission . . .

. . . the New Testament can be considered an attempt to answer in advance all the Cains of the world by softening the harsh outlines of God's face and by installing an intercessor between Him and man. Christ came to solve two principal problems, evil and death, which are precisely the problems that give rise to rebels. His solution consisted first of all in assuming them himself. The God–Man also suffers, but with patience. Neither evil nor death can any longer be unequivocally imputed to Him since He Himself suffers and dies. The night of Golgotha holds so important a place in human history only because in those dark shadows the divinity, ostensibly abandoning his traditional privileges, lived to the ultimate, despair included, man's death anguish. Thus is explained the *Lama sabacthani* and the fearful doubt of Christ in agony. Agony would be of small consequence if it were sustained by eternal hope. For God to be a man, He had to despair . . .

But from the moment Christianity, having passed beyond its triumphant period, was submitted to the critique of reason, to the exact extent that the divinity of Jesus was denied, pain and sorrow became once again the lot of men. Jesus undeified is only one more innocent whom the representatives of the God of Abraham tortured in a spectacular manner. The abyss that separated the master from the slaves opens once again and revolt raises anew its outcry toward the impenetrable face of a jealous God . . .
(*L'Homme révolté, PL/II*, pp. 435–46.)

1951

The Consequences of the "Death of God"

[*Camus sums up here, not dispassionately, some of Nietzsche's essential ideas. He had long since detached himself from Nietzsche's thought and rejected the latter's amor fati. But there is in this text a certain undeniable vibration: Camus had hung a photograph of Nietzsche in his study.*]

In this world rid of God and moral idols man is now alone and without a master. No one less than Nietzsche—and in this he may be distinguished from the Romantics—has allowed us to think that such great freedom could be easy. This savage deliverance puts him in the ranks of those whom he himself said suffered from a new form of anguish and a new form of happiness. But, at the beginning, it is his anguish alone that cries out: "Alas, grant me madness . . . Unless I am above the law I am the lowest of outcasts among all outcasts." Who cannot order his existence above the law must seek a new law or end in madness. From the moment when man no longer believes in God or in immortality, he becomes "responsible for everything that lives, for everything which, born in pain and sorrow, is destined to suffer from life." Upon him and him alone falls the task of discovering order and law. Then begins the era of the outcasts, the exhausting search for justifications, the aimless nostalgia, "the most painful, the most agonizing question: that of the heart that asks itself, 'Where will I ever be able to feel at home?'" . . .

. . . Without law freedom is not possible. If human

destiny is not oriented by some superior value, if chance is king, we are confronted with the march into darkness, the terrible freedom of the blind. At the opposite end of the highest form of deliverance, Nietzsche chose, then, the most extreme form of dependence. "If we do not make of the death of God a great renunciation and a perpetual victory over ourselves, we shall have to pay dearly for that loss." In other words, with Nietzsche revolt is transformed into asceticism. A more profound logic then replaces the "if nothing is true, everything is permissible" of Ivan Karamazov by an "if nothing is true, nothing is permissible." To deny that any one thing in this world is forbidden comes down to renouncing what is permissible. At the point where no man can any longer say what is black and what is white, the light is extinguished and freedom becomes a voluntary prison . . .

. . . The profound import of Nietzsche's thought is that the necessity of phenomena, if it is absolute, without weaknesses, implies absolutely no kind of restraint. Total adhesion to a total necessity: such is his paradoxical definition of freedom. The question "free from what?" is then replaced by "free for what"? Freedom coincides with heroism. It is the asceticism of the great man, "the most tightly drawn bow of them all." (*L'Homme révolté, P II*, pp. 479–82.)

Revolt and Generosity

[*Between Christian Hope and the secular faith in History, both equally illusory according to Camus and, in his eyes, inhuman in the final analysis, is Revolt, which is man's generous defense and his solidarity with the humiliated and the suffering.*]

There is without doubt an evil that men accrue in their frantic desire for unity. But yet another evil is at the origin of this chaotic passion. In the face of this evil, in the face of death, man from the depths of his being cries out for justice. Historical Christianity responds to this protest against evil only by proclaiming the kingdom, and then eternal life, both of which require faith. But suffering exhausts hope and faith; then it alone remains, isolated, without explanation. The working masses, worn out with suffering and dying, are masses without a god. Our place, then, is at their side, far from the old and the new teachers. Historical Christianity places beyond the pale of history the redress of evil and murder, which are nonetheless suffered within the course of history. Contemporary materialism also thinks it responds to these problems. But, as the servant of history it enlarges the domain of historical slaughter and at the same time leaves it unjustified, or else projects its justification into the future which again demands faith. In either case, it is necessary to wait, and, during this time, the innocent never cease dying. Over twenty centuries the sum total of evil in the world has not diminished. No Second Coming, divine or revolutionary, has occurred. An injustice remains attached to all suffering, even that which men consider the most deserved. Prometheus' long silence before the forces that torment him still cries out. Yet Prometheus, in the meantime, has seen mankind turn against him and ridicule him. Caught between human evil and destiny, between terror and the arbitrary, he retains only his force of revolt as a means of saving from death what can yet be saved without ceding to the arrogance of blasphemy . . .

We see then that revolt cannot do without a strange kind of love. Those who find their repose neither in God nor in

history are self-condemned to live for those who like themselves cannot live: for the downtrodden. The purest sentiment of revolt is thus crowned by the piercing cry of Ivan
Karamazov: if they cannot all be saved what good is the
salvation of a single one of them! Thus, condemned Catholics, in the dungeons of Spain, today refuse communion
because the priests loyal to the regime make it obligatory in
certain prisons. These too, lone witnesses to innocence crucified, refuse salvation if it must be paid for by injustice and
oppression. This reckless generosity is that of revolt which
gives without hesitation its strength of love and without
reservation gives the lie to injustice. Its honor lies in its
generous candor, in its giving all to the life of the moment
and to one's living brothers. In this way it showers blessings
on men yet to come. True generosity toward the future
consists in giving everything to the present. (*L'Homme
Révolté, PL/II,* pp. 706–707.)

1956

Jesus Betrayed by the Christians

[*Clamence makes of Jesus a man like all men—guilty,
anguished, poorly loved, alone. Despite the ironic tone, one
senses the sympathy of the author for this humanized, fraternal Christ.*]

. . . God's only usefulness would be to guarantee innocence and I would see religion rather as a great laundry
establishment, which in fact it was, but only briefly, for
three years to be exact, and it was not called religion. Since
then, there is a soap shortage; our noses are running and we

wipe each other clean. We are all dunces, all chastised, let us spit on one another and, pop! into the *malconfort!** He wins who spits first, that's all. I'm going to tell you a big secret, friend. Don't spend your time waiting for the last judgment. It happens every day.

No, it's nothing. I shiver a bit in this damned dampness. Here we are, anyway. There. After you. But stay a while, please, and accompany me. I haven't finished with it, I must continue. Continuing, that's what is difficult. Say, do you know why they crucified him, the other one, the one you're thinking about right now perhaps? Good, there are quantities of reasons for that. There are always reasons for a man's murder. It's impossible, on the contrary, to justify his living. That is why crime always has its advocates and innocence only sometimes. But besides those reasons which have been explained to us so well for the last two thousand years, there is one great reason for that horrible agony, and I do not know why it has been so carefully concealed. The real reason is that he knew, he did, that he was not completely innocent. If he didn't bear the burden of the crime he was accused of, he had committed others, even if he did not know which ones. Did he, in fact, not know them? He was at the source, after all; he must have heard about a certain massacre of the innocents. The children of Judea, massacred while his parents took him away to a safe place; why were they dead, if not because of him? He hadn't wished it, of course. Those bloody soldiers, those children cut in half, horrified him. But such as he was I am sure he could not forget them. And that sadness one senses in all his

* A *malconfort*, a "cell of little ease," was a medieval torture device consisting of a cage or small cell so constructed that the prisoner could neither stand up straight nor lie down at full length [trans. note].

acts, was it not the incurable melancholy of him who hears
throughout all the nights the voice of Rachel bewailing her
children and refusing all consolation? The plaint rose in the
night, Rachel called her children killed on his account, and
he was living!

Knowing what he knew, knowing all he did of mankind
—ah! who would have believed that crime lies not so much
in causing death as in not dying oneself—confronted day
and night with his innocent crime, it became too difficult
for him to hold on and continue. It was better to have done
with it, not defend himself, die, in order not to be the only
one left alive and to go elsewhere, some place where perhaps he would be justified. He was not justified, he complained of it, and to top it off they censored him. Yes, it was
the third evangelist, I believe, who began to tone down his
plaint, "Why hast thou forsaken me?" It was a seditious
cry, wasn't it? Well then, the scissors! Note moreover that
if Luke had suppressed nothing, the business would have
hardly been noticed; it wouldn't be so important in any
case. Thus the censor cries out the very thing he proscribes.
The order of the world is likewise ambiguous.

It doesn't matter that the censored man was not able to
continue. And I know, friend, what I'm talking about.
There was a time when at each minute I didn't know how I
would reach the next. Yes, one can make war in this world,
counterfeit love, torture one's fellow man, show off in the
newspapers, or simply speak ill of one's neighbor over one's
knitting. But, in certain cases, to continue, simply to continue, that's what is superhuman. And he was not superhuman, you can take my word for it. He cried out his agony
and that is why I admire him, my friend, who died without
knowing.

The unfortunate thing is that he left us alone, to continue, whatever happens, while we squat in our *malconfort*, knowing in our turn what he knew, but incapable of doing what he did and of dying as he did. People have tried, of course, to draw some solace from his death. After all, it was a stroke of genius to say to us: "You aren't any shining lights, all right, that's a fact. Ah well, we're not going to quibble about it. We're going to take care of that at a stroke, on the cross." But now, too many people climb up on to the cross only so they can be seen from farther away, even if they have to trample just a bit on him, who has been there for so long. Too many people have decided to dispense with generosity in order to practice charity. Oh, the injustice, the injustice that has been done him wrings my heart!

Ah! There I go, falling back into old habits, I'm going to plead for the defense. Pardon me, understand that I have my reasons. Listen, a few streets from here, there is a museum called "Our Lord of the Garret." At that period they built their catacombs in attics. What else could they do, the cellars here are flooded. But today, you can be sure, their Lord is no longer in the attic, nor in the cellar. They have perched him up in a judge's seat, in the secrecy of their hearts, and they strike hard; above all they judge, they judge in his name. He spoke gently to the adultress, "Neither do I condemn thee!" That doesn't stop them, they condemn, they absolve no one. In the name of the Lord, and you've had it. Lord? He didn't ask for so much as that, my friend. He wanted to be loved, no more than that. Certainly, there are people who love him, even among the Christians. But they are easily counted. He had foreseen that, moreover; he had a sense of humor. Peter, you know, the coward, Peter, then, denies him: "I do not know that man . . . I don't know what you mean . . . etc." Really, he did overdo it! And he makes a pun on Peter's name: "upon this rock I shall build my church." One couldn't be much more ironical, don't you agree. But no, they still manage to triumph! "You see, he had said it!" He had said it certainly, he understood the question very well. And then he left forever, leaving them to judge and to condemn, with pardon on their lips and condemnation in their hearts. (*La Chute*, *P/I*, pp. 1530–33.)

1957

Cosmic Ecstasy in the Immensity of Nature

[*Janine and her husband, an Algiers shopkeeper, are on a selling trip in southern Algeria. For the first time this woman, disappointed in life and old before her time, comes face to face with the desert.*]

As they ascended, the space before them widened and they made their way up into an ever more vast, cold and dry light where each noise from the oasis below reached them with distinct clarity. The illuminated air seemed to vibrate around them with an ever expanding vibration as they advanced, as if their passage struck off the crystalline air a sound wave that grew as it traveled out into space. And at the moment when, having reached the terrace, their gaze suddenly lost itself beyond the palm grove in the immense horizon, it seemed to Janine that the entire sky reverberated with a single thunderous, brief note whose echo little by little filled the space above her, then abruptly ceased, leaving her struck with silence before the limitless expanse . . .

Janine, her entire weight resting on the parapet, remained speechless, unable to tear herself from the emptiness that opened up before her. At her side, Marcel fretted. He was cold, he wanted to go back down. What was there to see up here? But she could not turn her gaze from the horizon. Out there, still farther to the south, at that point where the sky and the earth joined in a pure line, out there, it suddenly seemed to her, something was waiting for her which she had not known of until this day but which she had never ceased to miss. In the advancing afternoon the light was growing gently softer; it was changing from crystal to liquid. Meanwhile, in the heart of a woman whom chance alone had led to this spot, a knot tightened by the years, habit, and boredom slowly loosened. She looked at the Nomad's encampment. She had not caught sight of the men who lived there, nothing moved between the black tents, and yet she could think of nothing else but them, of whose existence she had scarcely been aware until that day. Having no houses, cut off from the world, they were a mere handful of wanderers upon the vast territory that she was exploring with her eyes, and which was nonetheless only a paltry part of a still greater space whose dizzying flight only came to an end thousands of kilometers farther to the south, there where the first great river gave birth to the thick forest. Since the beginning of time, on this arid soil, stripped clean to the bone, of this boundless land, men had been making their way without surcease, men who possessed nothing but who served no one, wretched and free overlords of a strange kingdom. Janine did not know why that idea filled her with a sadness so gentle and so immense that she had to shut her eyes. She only knew that this kingdom, for all time, had been promised her and that never, however, would it be hers, never again, except for that fleeting moment perhaps when she opened her eyes again upon the suddenly immobile sky with its streams of transfixed light, while the voices that rose from the Arab town abruptly fell silent. It seemed to her that the world's course had stopped just then and that from that instant on no one would grow old or die. Henceforth life was suspended everywhere except in her heart, within which, at that very moment, someone wept out of pain and awe. ("La Femme adultère," *P/I*, pp. 1567–68.)

Chronology

1913 Camus is born on November 7 at Mondovi, Department of Constantine, Algeria, where he is baptized. His father, a warehouse worker at a winery, is of Alsatian origin and of Christian background. His mother, Catherine Sintès, of Spanish descent, is Catholic but has "lapsed." His grandmother is a Catholic who practices out of a sense of tradition.

1914 In September, Camus's father is killed in the Battle of the Marne. His mother moves to the sordid Belcourt quarter of Algiers.

1918 to 1923 Camus, with his older brother, Lucien, attends the public elementary school in the rue Aumerat. For two of these years he also attends Thursday catechism classes at the parish church.

1923 Thanks to his teacher, Louis Germain, Camus obtains a scholarship to attend the *lycée*. His grandmother persuades the local pastor to allow Camus to make his first communion at the end of the 1922–1923 school year, before he enters the *lycée*.

1923 to 1930 Camus attends the Algiers *lycée* as a scholarship student. During this period he ceases to practice any religious faith.

1929 Camus has his first contact with philosophy. Jean Grenier is the teacher.

1930   Camus enters the final year at the *lycée*—the "philoso-
       phy year"—again with Jean Grenier as his teacher.
       He suffers his first attack of tuberculosis.

1933   Jean Grenier publishes *Les Iles*. Camus registers at the
       Faculty of Letters and Sciences of the University of
       Algiers, where he prepares his dgree of *Licence ès
       Lettres* in philosophy.
       Hitler assumes power in Germany.

1934   In a civil ceremony, Camus marries Simone Hie, daugh-
       ter of an Algiers physician.
       Under the direction of Professor René Poirier, Camus
       undertakes the study of modern philosophy (Kierke-
       gaard, Husserl, Heidegger).

1935   Divorce. He leads a very independent and rather irregu-
       lar existence.
       Camus joins the Communist Party at the end of 1934
       and devotes himself to propaganda work among the
       Moslems.
       He begins *L'Envers et l'endroit*, founds the "Théâtre du
       Travail" in collaboration with a group of young work-
       ers, and finishes his *Licence* in philosophy.

1936   He completes his thesis (*Métaphysique chrétienne et
       Néoplatonisme*) for the Diplôme d'Etudes Supérieures.
       This work introduces Camus to Christian philosophy,
       and in it one can sense his hesitation between Greek
       serenity and Christian anguish.
       March: Germany reoccupies the Rhineland. Camus fin-
       ishes his first play, *Révolte dans les Asturies*, a political
       work but in no way anticlerical.
       May: Success of the Popular Front. The Civil War
       breaks out in Spain.
       Summer: Camus travels in Central Europe.

1937   He is unable, for reasons of health, to continue work
       toward a higher degree in the University.
       He breaks with the Communist Party and aligns himself
       with Messali Hadj's Mouvement de Libération Nation-
       ale, an Algerian nationalist party.
       He turns down a teaching position at Sidi-bel-Abbès.

1938   Camus is a journalist for *Alger-Républicain*, a daily he
        helped Pascal Pia to found.

1939   Camus goes to Kabylia to write a report for *Alger-Ré-
        publicain* on the famine gripping the region.
        September 3: War is declared. Camus tries to enlist but
        is turned down for health reasons.
        Alger-Républicain is closed by the censorship office.
        Camus goes to Paris. He works for a time on the staff of
        Paris-Soir but is not happy with his job.
        May: *L'Etranger*, begun in 1937, is completed. The
        Germans invade France.

1940   Camus enters into his second civil marriage, this time
        with an Oranaise, Francine Faure, who will bear him
        twin children.

1941   Camus returns to Oran and works there as a teacher in a
        collège. *Le Mythe de Sisyphe*, begun in 1938, is com-
        pleted.

1942   A new bout with tuberculosis and a return to France.
        L'Etranger is published and work is begun on *La Peste*.
        Camus enters into a resistance organization, "Combat,"
        where he meets Claude Bourdet, who will later succeed
        him as editor of the Parisian daily *Combat*.

1943   *Le Mythe de Sisyphe* is published; the first version of
        Le Malentendu and the first *Lettre à un ami allemand*
        are written; and in *Les Cahiers du sud* (April) he pub-
        lishes a review of Jean Guitton's book on Father
        Pouget, a work that Camus had found to be quite
        interesting.

1944   Camus meets with Sartre.
        The second *Lettre à un ami allemand* is written.
        Camus assumes the editorship of *Combat*, with Pascal
        Pia as his managing editor.
        Le Malentendu is staged, with Maria Casarès as Marthe.

1945   *Caligula* is produced at the Théâtre Herbetot.

1946   Camus reads the works of Simone Weil, several of
        which he will be responsible for having published at
        Gallimard.

Invited by the Dominicans of Latour-Maubourg, he gives a lecture on "L'Incroyant et les Chrétiens."

1947 Uprisings in Madagascar and Algeria are repressed by the French government. The Indo-Chinese war begins. June: *La Peste* is published with great success.

The team Camus had formed to run *Combat* breaks up; some members join the Gaullist Rassemblement du Peuple Français, others the Socialists. Camus resigns and turns the editorship over to Claude Bourdet.

1948 There is a Communist coup in Prague. Yugoslavia is expelled from the Cominform.

Camus writes *L'Etat de Siège* and *Les Justes*.

September: Camus makes a very mysterious stay in the Dominican monastery of Saint-Maximin. Upon his return, on September 20, he writes to his friend Francis Ponge, a poet and (then) a Communist, that he found in the monastery "the interior silence he needed" and undertakes a kind of apologetic for Christianity: "One must not judge a doctrine on its by-products, but on its summits" (*Essais*, p. 1596).*

---

* Onimus includes a reference here which is unclear. He writes: "The friendship of Father Bruckberger (cf. *Essais*, p. 176 [an obviously incorrect citation]) and of the Christian poet René Leynaud, friend of Francis Ponge and journalist at Lyons (killed by the collaborationist Milice in 1944). Leynaud embodied for Camus the model of the sincere Christian, passionate and pure, who dies as a martyr for his commitment." Having been killed in 1944, René Leynaud was of course already dead in 1948. Father Bruckberger was very much alive, however, and he was most likely responsible for Camus's "mysterious" visit to the monastery, which was probably made for the purpose of getting some rest and gathering his strength, the difficulties of editing *Combat*, and the final breakup of the team he had formed to run the paper, having reduced Camus to near-exhaustion in 1947. Roger Quilliot sees nothing mysterious in the visit, be it noted, and the lengthier fragments he cities from Camus's correspondence with Ponge with regard to Christianity reiterates more explicitly Camus's continuing rejection of any personal religious belief than the fragmentary citation given by M. Onimus indicates [trans. note].

1949   The Rajk Trial in Hungary. Camus makes an appeal in behalf of Greek Communists condemned to death.
Camus makes a trip to South America.
Ill once again, Camus is obliged to curtail his activities.
Les Justes is produced in December.

1951   *L'Homme révolté* is published.

1952   Francis Jeanson's article attacking *L'Homme révolté* appears in Sartre's *Les Temps modernes* (May), followed by Camus's own counter-reply. He makes a definitive break with Sartre.
November: Camus resigns from UNESCO to protest Spain's admission to that body.

1954   *L'Eté* is published.

1955   In *L'Express*, Camus publishes articles on the North African problem.

1956   January: Camus, in Algiers, makes an appeal for a truce.
May: *La Chute* is published.
Summer: Camus's adaptation of Faulkner's *Requiem for a Nun* is staged.
November: Insurrection in Hungary. Camus takes part in a protest meeting against the intervention of Russian tanks.

1957   March: *L'Exil et le royaume* is published.
November: Camus is awarded the Nobel Prize for Literature. In an interview given on this occasion, Camus sums up thus his position with regard to Christianity: "I have only veneration and respect for the person of Christ and for his life. I do not believe in his resurrection" (*Essais*, p. 1597).

1958   Camus, who had first visited Loumarin in 1947, buys a house in this small out-of-the-way Provençal town.

1959   Camus' stage adaptation of Dostoevski's *The Possessed* is produced.

1960   On January 4, Camus is killed in an auto accident on the way from Loumarin to Paris.

Select Bibliography

[I have included here primarily the books and articles M. Onimus listed in the original French study; the only modifications of his listings are separation of French-language items from those in English and rearrangement of the entries in alphabetical rather than chronological order. I have also added page references for those items reprinted in the two-volume Pléiade edition of Camus's work (*P/I* and *PL/II*). The occasional critical comments, unless otherwise indicated, are M. Onimus's. I have added a listing of English translations of Camus's major works. For the most complete bibliographical data on Camus and his work, including translations into all languages, I refer the reader to Professor Robert F. Roeming's monumental work: *Camus: A Bibliography* (Madison: University of Wisconsin Press, 1968) (trans. note).]

FRENCH-LANGUAGE WORKS

Works by Camus
Camus's complete works, including his theatrical adaptations, comprise twenty-five volumes published between 1937 and 1958. (For original publication dates of individual works, see the "Chronology" elsewhere in this volume.) All of these works with the exception of *L'Envers et l'endroit* (Algiers: Charlot, 1937) appeared originally under the Gallimard im-

print, and Gallimard also reprinted *L'Envers et l'endroit* in 1958. All of Camus's published works in French, along with much valuable supplementary documentation, have been collected in the following two-volume critical edition under the direction of Roger Quilliot:

Théâtre, récits, nouvelles. Paris: Gallimard (Editions de la Pléiade), 1962.

Essais. Paris: Gallimard (Editions de la Pléiade), 1965.

Selected Articles by Camus

The following articles bear directly upon the subject of the present study:

"Lettre à Bernanos," *Bulletin de la Société des Amis de Bernanos,* No. 45 (March, 1962).

"Lettre au Directeur," *Dieu vivant* (May 28, 1952), (*PL/II,* pp. 744–45).

"Lettre au sujet du 'Parti pris,' " *La Nouvelle revue française* No. 45 (September, 1956), (*PL/II,* pp. 1662–68).

"Nietzsche et le nihilisme," *Les Temps modernes,* No. 70 (August, 1951). [This article appears as a chapter in *L'Homme révolté* (trans. note).]

"Pessimisme et action," *Fiches d'Information du Centre Universitaire Catholique* (June 13, 1945).

"Portrait d'un élu," *Cahiers du sud,* No. 225 (April, 1943), (*PL/II,* pp. 1597–1603).

"Remarques sur la révolte," in *L'Existence.* Ed. Jean Grenier. Paris: Gallimard, 1945 (*PL/II,* pp. 1682–97).

Selected Works with Prefaces by Camus

Grenier, Jean. *Les Iles.* Paris: Gallimard, 1955 (*PL/II,* pp. 1157–61).

Leynaud, René. *Poésies posthumes.* Paris: Gallimard, 1947 (*PL/II,* pp. 1471–79).

Martin du Gard, Roger. *Œuvres complètes.* Paris: Gallimard, 1955 (*PL/II,* pp. 1131–55).

Melville, Herman. *Moby Dick.* Paris: Gallimard, 1955 (*P/I,* pp. 1899–1903).

Weil Simone. *L'Enracinement.* This preface was never actually included in the edition of Weil's work, but has been printed in *PL/II,* p. 1700.

Important Interviews Given by Camus
   Les Nouvelles littéraires, Nov. 15, 1945 (*PL/II*, pp. 1424–27).
   Le Littéraire, Aug. 10, 1946.
   La Revue du Caire, 1948 (*PL/II*, pp. 379–83).
   Les Nouvelles littéraires, May 10, 1951.
   Gazette des lettres, Feb. 15, 1952 (*PL/II*, pp. 737–43).
   Gazette de Lausanne, Mar. 15, 1954 (*PL/II*, pp. 1836–38).
   Le Monde, Aug. 31, 1956 (*P I*, pp. 1870–72).
   Demain, Oct. 24–30, 1957 (*P II*, pp. 1898–1904).
   Occidente, LIV, No. 237.
   Venture, III, pp. 26–40 (*Venture* is an American publication
   (New York) and the interview originally appeared in
   English; a French translation appears in *P II*, 1925–28).

Books on Camus and his Work
   Brisville, Jean-Claude. *Camus*. Paris: Gallimard, 1959. A
   very useful introduction with a short biography and a
   bibliography.
   Durand, Anne. *Le Cas Albert Camus*. Paris: Fischbacher,
   1961. Interesting information of Camus's youth by an
   Algerian who knew him. [It is not at all certain that Mme.
   Durand "knew" Camus in Algeria, although she does pro-
   fess to know the surroundings in which he grew up. The
   author bitterly opposes Camus's political views, especially
   with regard to Algeria, and the book is quite strongly
   biased in its entirety (trans. note).]
   Gélinas, Germain-Paul. *La Liberté dans la pensée de Camus*.
   Fribourg: Editions Universitaires, 1965. A rather unsyste-
   matic study.
   Ginestier, Paul. *Pour connaître la pensée de Camus*. Paris:
   Bordas, 1964. Especially valuable for the texts cited.
   Lebesque, Morvan. *Camus par lui-même*. Paris: Seuil, 1963.
   Especially valuable for the documents it contains.
   Majault, Joseph. *Camus*. Paris: Le Centurion, 1965.
   Papamalamis, Dimitris. *Albert Camus et la pensée grecque*.
   Nancy: Université de Nancy, 1965. Informative but un-
   methodical.
   Quilliot, Roger. *La Mer et les prisons*. Paris: Gallimard,
   1956. An excellent biography. [M. Quilliot's book is due

to appear in a revised edition in 1970; an English translation of the revised edition is in preparation under the
direction of the University of Alabama Press (trans.
note).]

Simon, Pierre-Henri. *Présence de Camus*. Paris: La Renais-
sance du Livre, 1962.

Van-Huy, Nguyen. *La Métaphysique du bonheur chez Albert Camus*. Neuchâtel: La Baconnière, 1964. Contains an
excellent bibliography.

Articles on Camus and His Work

Barjon, L., "Le Silence de Dieu dans la littérature contempo-
raine," *Etudes* (May, 1954).

Beigbeder, Marc, "Le Monde n'est pas absurde," *Esprit*, No.
3 (1945). The protest of a believer.

Berl, Emmanuel, "lettre à Albert Camus," *La Table ronde*
(July, 1956).

Bespaloff, Rachel, "Le Monde du condamné à mort," *Esprit*
(January, 1950). A critical essay and synthesis.

Blanchet, A., *La Littérature et le spirituel*, III. Paris: Aubier,
1961.

Bruckberger, Marc, *"La Peste,"* Le Cheval de Troie, No. 2
(1947). A Christian statement concerning Paneloux.

Carrouges, Michel, "Philosophie de la *Peste*," *Vie intellectuelle* (July, 1947).

Conilh, Jean, "L'Exil sans royaume," *Esprit* (April-May,
1958). Penetrating analysis of atheist alienation.

De Boisdeffre, P., "L'Evolution spirituelle de Camus," *Eccle-
sia* (August, 1957). A very penetrating sketch.

Doubrovsky, Serge, "La Morale d'Albert Camus," *Preuves*,
No. 116 (October, 1960).

Du Rostu, Jean, "Un Pascal sans Christ," *Etudes* (October
and November, 1945). A very important and penetrating
study.

Espiau de la Maëstre, A., "Albert Camus, pèlerin de
l'Absolu," *Les Lettres romanes*, XV (1961), pp. 1-22.

————, "Albert Camus und das Christentum," *Der grosse
Entschluss* (November-December, 1958).

Jeanson, Francis, "Albert Camus ou l'âme révoltée," *Les
Temps modernes*, No. 79 (May, 1952), pp. 2070-90.

———, "Pour tout vous dire," *Les Temps modernes* (August, 1952), pp. 354–83.

Lepp, I. "L'Athéisme désespéré de Camus," in *Psychanalyse de l'athéisme moderne* (1961).

Martin, A. G., "Camus et le Christianisme," *La Revue réformée*, No. 4 (1961).

Moeller, Charles, "Existentialisme et pensée chrétienne," *La Revue nouvelle* (June, 1951).

Moré, Marcel, "L'Homme révolté," *Dieu vivant* (April, 1952).

Mounier, Emmanuel, "Camus parle," *Esprit*, No. 15 (1947).

Onimus, J., "A. Camus et le mystère de la foi," *Cahiers universitaires catholiques* (December, 1957).

———, "*Caligula* ou la tragédie de l'intelligence," *Etudes* (June, 1958).

———, "Camus, la femme adultère et le ciel étoilé," *Cahiers universitaires catholiques* (July, 1960).

———, "*La Chute*," *Cahiers universitaires catholiques* (October, 1956).

Picon, G. *Usage de la lecture*, II. Paris: Gallimard, 1962.

Roynet, L., "Un incroyant chez les chrétiens," *Vie intellectuelle* (April, 1949). Notes taken during Camus's speech to the Dominicans of Latour-Maubourg.

Sartre, Jean-Paul, "Réponse à Albert Camus," *Les Temps modernes*, No. 82 (August, 1952), pp. 334–53.

Simon, P.-H., "Albert Camus devant le péché," *Témoignage chrétien* (June 15, 1956).

———, "Albert Camus entre Dieu et l'Histoire," *Terre humaine* (February, 1952).

Special Numbers of Reviews Devoted to Camus

Albert Camus devant la critique anglo-saxonne, Revue des lettres modernes (Paris: Minard, 1961). Extremely useful.

Albert Camus devant la critique allemande, Revue des Lettres modernes (Paris: Minard, 1963). Extremely useful.

La Nouvelle Revue française, Numéro Spécial (March, 1960).

La Table ronde, Numéro Spécial (February, 1960). Contains important contributions from J. Guitton, G. Marcel, Marill-Albérès, J. Madaule, etc.

ENGLISH-LANGUAGE WORKS

Translations of Camus's Works
  Caligula and Three Other Plays (*The Misunderstanding* [*Le
    Malentendu*], *State of Siege* [*L'Etat de siège*], and *The
    Just Assassins* [*Les Justes*]). Trans. Stuart Gilbert. New
    York: Knopf, 1958.
  Exile and the Kingdom [*L'Exil et le royaume*]. Trans. Justin
    O'Brien. New York, Knopf, 1957. (This work and *The
    Fall* have been printed in one volume in a Modern Library
    Edition.)
  The Fall [*La Chute*]. Trans. Justin O'Brien. New York;
    Knopf, 1956.
  Lyrical and Critical Essays [*Noces, L'Eté, L'Envers et
    l'endroit* along with critical essays on various writers in-
    cluding Sartre, Silone, Melville, Gide and Faulkner].
    Trans. Ellen Conroy Kennedy. New York: Knopf, 1968.
  The Myth of Sisyphus (*Le Mythe de Sisyphe*). Trans.
    Justin O'Brien. New York, Knopf, 1955.
  Notebooks: 1935–42 (*Carnets*). Trans. Philip Thody. New
    York: Knopf, 1963. (Also in Modern Library.)
  The Plague (*La Peste*). Trans. Stuart Gilbert. New York:
    Knopf, 1948. (Also in Vintage paperback.)
  The Possessed [*Les Possédés*]. Trans. Justin O'Brien. New
    York: Knopf, 1960.
  The Rebel [*L'Homme révolté*]. Trans. Anthony Bower.
    New York: Knopf, 1954. (Also in Vintage paperback.)
  Resistance, Rebellion and Death [*Lettres à un ami allemand*,
    Réflexions sur la guillotine, and selected articles and es-
    says, most of them from *Actuelles*]. Trans. Justin O'Brien.
    New York: Knopf, 1960. (Also in Modern Library.)
  The Stranger (*L'Étranger*). Trans. Stuart Gilbert. New
    York: Knopf, 1946. (Also in Vintage paperback.)
  *Speech of Acceptance upon the Award of the Nobel Prize
    for Literature* [*Discours de Suède*]. Trans. Justin O'Brien.
    New York: Knopf, 1958. (Also printed in *The Atlantic*
    [May 1958], pp. 33–34.)

Books on Camus and His Work

Brée, Germaine. *Camus* (rev. ed.). New Brunswick: Rutgers University Press, 1961. The author knew Camus personally and had the manuscript of *La Mort heureuse* at her disposal.

Cruickshank, John. *Albert Camus and the Literature of Revolt*. New York: Oxford University Press, 1960. An excellent synthesis.

Hanna, Thomas. *The Thought and Art of Albert Camus*. Chicago: Henry Regnery Co., 1958. A treatment of Camus by a Protestant theologian.

Parker, Emmett. *Albert Camus: The Artist in the Arena*. Madison: The University of Wisconsin Press, 1965. [A study of Camus as a journalist and *artiste engagé* (trans. note).]

Roeming, Robert F. *Camus: A Bibliography*. Madison: The University of Wisconsin Press, 1968. [A most excellent and complete bibliography of writings by Camus and on him and his work; this bibliography supersedes all previous ones on Camus (trans. note).]

Thody, Philip. *Albert Camus: A Study of His Work*. New York: Grove Press, 1959.

———. *Albert Camus: 1913–1960*. London: Hamish-Hamilton, 1961. This work is by far the best and the most profound we have read on Camus's thought. [I am sorry to have to disagree with M. Onimus's superlative assessment of this book. While there is much of great value in it, Mr. Thody makes some judgments not shared by all Camus scholars. The beginning student of Camus would do well to consult both the Brée and Cruickshank studies in English and Roger Quilliot's *La Mer et les prisons* in French before drawing any definitive conclusions with regard to Camus's thought (trans. note).]

Articles on Camus and His Work

Frohock, W. M., "Camus: Image, Influence and Sensibility," *Yale French Studies*, No. 2 (1949), pp. 91–99. A bit rapid but a remarkable conclusion.

Hanna, Thomas, "Albert Camus and the Christian Faith," *The Journal of Religion*, XXXVI, No. 4 (October, 1956),

pp. 224–33. A Protestant theologian's very sympathetic
reaction. [This article is reprinted in *Camus: A Collection
of Critical Essays* (see below) (trans. note).]

Loose, John, "The Christian as Camus's Absurd Man," *The
Journal of Religion*, XLII (October, 1962), pp. 203–14.

Symposium, XII, Nos. 1, 2 (Spring-Fall, 1958). Several important articles on Camus including Germaine Brée's
"Camus' *Caligula:* Evolution of a Play," pp. 43–51.

[In addition to the foregoing items cited by M. Onimus, the
reader might wish to consult the special number of *Yale
French Studies* (Spring, 1960) devoted to Camus, as well as an
excellent general selection of articles on Camus contained in
Camus: A Collection of Critical Essays, ed. Germaine Brée
(Englewood Cliffs, N.J.: Prentice-Hall, 1962). Besides Mr.
Roeming's very complete bibliography mentioned above, the
Brée, Cruickshank, and Parker studies, cited above, contain
extensive bibliographical listings of English-language articles
on Camus (trans. note).]

Index

1. Camus's Works

Actuelles, 36 n., 84, 90, 119
Avenir de la tragédie, 5

Caligula, 15–16, 30, 70–73,
    100, 104
Carnets, 19–20, 26, 29, 45–46,
    57, 65, 69–70, 88, 102
La Chute, 8, 16, 26–27, 30, 39,
    50, 68, 71, 91–97, 99–101,
    141

L'Envers et l'endroit, 16–17,
    18, 20, 24, 26, 28, 32 n.,
    33, 93–94, 103, 107–108
L'État de Siège, 91, 105
L'Été, 11, 14, 15, 18, 78, 79,
    85, 93, 106
L'Étranger, 8, 17, 29, 34, 66–
    67, 70, 110–115
L'Exil et le royaume, 12, 13,
    48, 95

L'Homme révolté, 18, 38, 39,
    49, 50, 76, 83, 87, 88, 89,
    90, 104–105, 129–130,
    131–133, 134–137

Les Justes, 81–83, 85, 88–89

Lettres à un ami allemand, 39,
    77, 79–80

Le Malentendu, 11, 51–52, 68
Métaphysique chrétienne et
    néoplatonisme, 17–18, 54
La Mort heureuse, 28, 69–70
Le Mythe de Sisyphe, 21, 25,
    30, 43, 49, 57, 58, 65, 69,
    73–76, 104

Noces, 8 n., 11, 13, 17, 27, 40,
    41–42, 44, 65, 66, 86, 102

La Peste, 19, 20, 25, 34, 45–
    47, 48, 52, 57, 62, 86, 87,
    94, 119–128

2. Names of Persons

Abraham, 49, 57, 133
Acault, 35
Anouilh, 24
Arland, 101
Augustine, St., 53, 54, 56, 101,
    102, 105, 115

Barrès, 19
Beauvoir, 82, 85, 91–92, 95
Bernanos, 98, 99
Brisville, 12
Buffet, 68

Chestov, 57
Claudel, 34–35, 63
Copernicus, 118

D'Annunzio, 19
Descartes, 7
Dostoevski, 9, 10, 12, 16, 24,
    28, 38 n., 45, 58, 73, 100
Durand, 2 n.

Epictetus, 27

Feuerbach, 40
Freud, 100

Galileo, 118
Gallimard, 60
Gide, 35, 41
Grenier, 9, 11, 21–22, 25, 37,
    52, 53, 66
Guitton, 36, 39, 55, 115

Hegel, 56, 90
Hugo, 51

Job, 46, 47, 124

Kafka, 73
Kant, 78
Kierkegaard, 53, 56, 57, 58,
    61, 102

Lubac, 56

Malraux, 23, 41, 74
Marcel, 76, 105
Marx, 82
Mauriac, 102
Melville, 23
Michaux, 85
Milosz, 87
Montherlant, 41, 74
Mounier, 74

Nietzsche, 36, 40, 59, 74, 75,
    77, 80, 90, 103, 104, 134

Pascal, 53, 55, 56, 62, 85, 117
Péguy, 3, 63
Plato, 60
Plotinus, 13, 54, 115
Poirier, 54
Proudhon, 40, 47, 86

Rembrandt, 7
Richaud, 25
Rousseau, 78

Saint-Exupéry, 87
Sartre, 14, 85, 97
Socrates, 84

Teilhard de Chardin, 63
Tertullian, 55
Tolstoi, 24

Vigny, 41

Weil, 60, 62

3. Topics

Absurd, 49, 55, 75, 76, 88, 104
Alienation, 48, 66
Antitheism, 45, 55, 130

Christ, 38, 49–50, 53, 59, 61, 98, 102, 133, 137–140
Christianity, 31–64, 129, 136
Conscience and Consciousness, 8, 21, 68–69, 97–98
Comic Ecstasy, 8–9, 44, 141–143

Death, 20, 27–29, 42, 45, 70, 108–109, 136
Dialogue, 84–88

Evil, 24, 43, 45, 48, 62, 70, 81, 94, 102, 118–119, 133, 136

Faith, 47, 56, 57, 103, 115–118

God, 33–34, 102–103, 104, 105, 106
Grace, 62
Greek Wisdom and Moderation, 7, 17–18, 37, 60, 85, 104
Guilt, 93, 96–97

Happiness, 72, 84, 91–92, 104
History, 4–5, 41, 80, 90, 106
Hope, 43, 44, 66, 73–74, 80, 106
Humanism, 64, 89, 92, 104

Innocence, 67, 89, 96, 137

Justice, 65, 82–83, 136, 137

Love, 17, 29, 56, 71, 88–89, 106

Moderation, 7, 17–18, 37, 60, 85, 104

Nihilism, 43, 64, 72, 78, 79–80, 83, 89, 105

Religion, 32–39, 40, 42, 107
Revolt, 38, 39, 64, 72, 90, 129–133, 135–137
Revolution, 81–82

Tragic, the, 7, 29, 74

RITTER LIBRARY
BALDWIN-WALLACE COLLEGE

Date Due

JE 2 '71
NO 3 '72
MR 13 '73
MY 3 '73
AL 10 13
DE 12 75
AG 27 '76
OC 27 '76
OCT 1982
NOV 1 3 1982
JAN 23 1983
FE Employee lips
JAN - 5 1987
JAN - 3 1987
MAR 10

WITHDRAWN

Demco 38-297